A SELECT COLOUR HANDBOOK

MODERN LOCOMOTIVES

SELECTA

First published in England 1994 by
Wordsworth Editions Ltd
Cumberland House
Crib Street
Ware
Hertfordshire SG12 9ET

ISBN 1-85326-812-7

Superlaunch Ltd thank the many manufacturers and
railway operators, particularly GEC Alsthom, for their
generous assistance with the production of this book

Designed and produced by Superlaunch Ltd
P O Box 207, Abingdon, Oxfordshire OX13 6TA, England
Text conversion and pagination by
August Filmsetting, St Helens, England
Colour separation by Seagull Reproductions Ltd, London
Printed and bound in the Czech Republic by Svoboda

CONTENTS

Below: **a diesel-electric locomotive of the State Railways of Ecuador (ENFE)**

Title page: **Canadian National's latest addition to its diesel locomotive fleet**

HISTORY

Steam power ruled supreme for more than a century, but today's locomotives are almost always diesel or electric, although some steam and some trains driven by gas turbines also exist. The challenge to steam began within a few years of *Rocket*'s success, when in 1835 a blacksmith named Thomas Davenport of Vermont, USA, patented his electric motor; he also built a model electric railway which still survives.

A full-size electric locomotive was first built in 1842 by a Scotsman called Robert Davidson, and it ran, although very slowly, on the Edinburgh & Glasgow Railway track. Electric traction was still impractical; the primary batteries used were by no means adequate for the job, and an efficient powerful source of energy was quite desperately required.

In 1860, an Italian, Antonio Pacinotti, supplied the answer when he built the first dynamo; this could also be used as an electric motor and is the basis of the vast majority of today's locomotives.

The arguments and developments that ensued are shown in the pages which follow, which depict the major changes in both diesel and electric motive power around the world. The debate centred on which kind of current to use, direct current (dc) which had proved the best for traction motors, or alternating current (ac) that provided better transmission; and where to put the expensive elements of the complicated machinery, aboard the locomotive or built into the supply system.

Some lines compromised, and used such very low-frequency alternating current that it was almost dc. Today, technological developments have solved the problem and simple conversion methods on the engines enable the supply to be ac and the motors to be dc.

The New York, New Haven & Hartford Railway electrified a section of its main line in 1907, using simple double-bogie (Bo-Bo) locomotives and also self-propelled passenger trains. They utilised single-phase alternating current and overhead catenary current supply, very similar to the method employed by railways today. Electric traction had proved itself, but owing to the vast expense involved when compared to steam – of the order of five times the outlay – steam continued to rule for a further

4

AEG single railcar
illustrated below

Country of origin: Germany
Railway: Study Group for
Electric High-Speed Railways
Date: 1901
Type: experimental railcar
Gauge: 1,435mm (54.56in)
Length overall: 22.1m (72ft 6in)
Total weight: 60 tonnes
(132,250lb)
Propulsion: three-phase
current variable between 10,000
and 14,000V with a frequency
variable between 38-40Hz, fed
via a triple overhead side-
contact wire and a step-down
transformer to six gearless
synchronous motors, each
having a capacity of 560kW
(750hp) for short periods

half-century, even although
speeds in excess of 160km/h (100
mph) were achieved in demon-
strations in Germany in 1901,
and in 1903, a single motor
coach reached a record speed of
210km/h (130.5mph), which was
to stand in Germany for over 70
years.

The story of the diesel locomotive also had a slow start. In
1896, the first Ackroyd-Stuart
type diesel locomotive was
built by Richard Hornsby & Co
in England 'in house', using an
internal combustion engine in
which the fuel was injected into
the cylinder by a blast of com-
pressed air at the end of the
piston stroke. This engine was
used for shunting duties at
Hornsby's works, whereas the

first engine to employ Dr Diesel's engine in public service appears to have been a small Swedish railcar with a 56kW (75hp) engine and with electrical transmission employed on the Mellersta & Södermanlunds Railway in 1913.

It was not, however, until 1924 that the first efficient diesel-electric locomotive was used successfully in real commercial service, using a diesel engine to drive an electric generator alternator which fed current to the motors. Again, like the early electric traction locomotives, this was expensive; in addition, it was also complex to build and the marriage of vibrating oil-covered diesel engines and electrical equipment was not usually a happy one.

The real assault on steam railways was made in the 1930s by General Motors, when it first offered an off-the-shelf standardised reliable unit that could be coupled up from a single unit for light duties to a superpower loco of, say, four units. Costs were reduced to an acceptable level, paying little attention to the tradition of locomotive design, but diesel traction had arrived.

It should also be mentioned that the development of gas-turbine power proved very

A series 200 trainset of Japan's Shinkansen line

practical in certain areas, though its application was never commonplace.

The switch to 'new' forms of driving power for the locomotive did not detract from the ever-present urgency to deliver from A to B, and even today the running speeds continue to increase. In 1966, the electric Shinkansen 'Bullet' trains from Japan captured the world's imagination. In 1978 it was the diesel-electric HST 125 trains in Britain that established city-to-city speeds of 160km/h (100mph); since when, the French electric *Train à Grande Vitesse* (TGV) has competed with the Japanese train for the world's fastest service, nearing 300km/h (186.3mph), while other nations strive to keep abreast of the demand for speed.

Technological developments add to the spectra of improved aerodynamic design, tilting trains that can navigate curves at high speeds, hover-trains and even magnetic levitation systems; all are deployed in a continual desire to go faster, cheaper, more safely and comfortably from A to B, in face of competition from the airways and road transport.

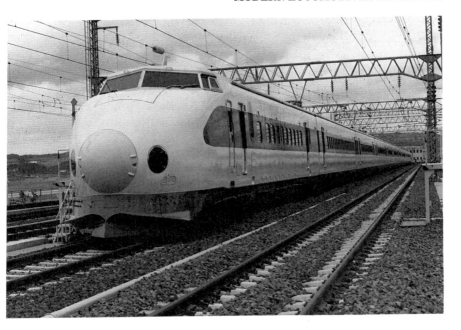

MOTIVE POWER

Although not always the case in its early days, today's electric motive power is normally carried on two-axle or three-axle bogies, and the most widely-applied electrification system is high-voltage direct current of 1,500V or 3,000V, although the cheapest method of main-line electrification is 25,000V single-phase, 50Hz or 60Hz alternating current.

Low-voltage direct current electrification is the cheapest form of railway electrification, but only when limited to a track system of less than 24km (15 miles) – a fact that seems to

have eluded British Rail, with its 1,600km (1,000-mile) network. The voltage used here is normally 750V; however, under Soviet influence some of the former Warsaw Pact countries used 825V.

Three-phase electrification, using two overhead contact wires, has disappeared with the exception of a very few mountain rack railways. Over the years, there have been many other forms of electrification, each developed to utilise the most up-to-date technology. Unfortunately, the cost of updating any electrified track is often prohibitively expensive, and for that reason 15,000V single-phase $16\frac{2}{3}$Hz is still in use in parts of Europe and 11,000V single-phase 25Hz alternating current in use in the USA. Electrification is usually most economical when the line carries a lot of traffic – in the former Soviet Union, this was calculated as in excess of one train each half hour. When a line carries less traffic, the diesel-powered locomotive is the more cost-efficient choice.

SJ Class D No 101, an early wooden-bodied version of this general-purpose rod-driven electric locomotive class. Some of the 417 built are still operated

Class D 1-C-1

Country of origin: Sweden
Railway: Swedish State Railways (SJ)
Date: 1925
Type: electric mixed-traffic locomotive
Gauge: 1,435mm (54.56in)
Total weight: 75 tonnes (165,300lb)
Propulsion: $16\frac{2}{3}$Hz (15,000V) single-phase current, fed via overhead catenary with step-down transformer to two 930kW (1,250hp) motors, which drive the wheels via gearing, jackshaft and connecting rods
Maximum axle load: 17 tonnes (37,600lb)
Tractive effort: 154kN (34,600lb)
Maximum speed: 100km/h (62mph)
History: the first Class D locomotives appeared in 1925, but upgraded variants were still being built in 1952. The Swedish electrification system basically followed that of Germany and Switzerland, but with supplies of electricity being taken from the national grid at normal frequency by rotary-converter sub-stations.

DIRECT CURRENT

This always flows from one point to the next in the same direction. By using a soft iron core or rod, around which many coils of insulated wire are wound and passing an electric current through the coils, the coils are made to act as a magnet. Pacinotti placed two of these electromagnets face-to-face in a frame known as the stator, with a further pair similarly arranged and placed on a shaft called the rotor, that rotated inside the stator.

The direction in which the electric current flows through the coils depends on which end of the electromagnet is the north pole, and which the south. By adopting the well-known principle of two like magnetic poles repelling each other, Pacinotti wired his motor so that the stator and rotor poles that faced each other had the same polarity: thus when the current was turned on, the shaft was forced to rotate. However, when the rotor shaft has rotated through 180°, the current would flow in the opposite direction, and so the polarity of the end of the core altered so that it now faced an opposite polarity of the stator electromagnet. Pacinotti overcame this prob-

lem by devising a commutator of two copper segments per electromagnet, which were mounted on the rotor shaft and maintained electrical contact by means of copper brushes. Each segment was carefully wired to the rotor poles and carefully insulated, but such was the wiring that the current flowed with its polarity in the opposite direction to that of the other pole, so that as the commutator turned together with the rotor poles, the current flow in the poles was reversed, right polarity maintained and the resultant movement was then ready for exploitation to drive a locomotive or other such machinery.

Needless to say, today's locomotive builders have managed to create a far more complex arrangement, but the majority of electric locomotives (and for that matter diesel-electrics) to be found in the world today use the series-wound (current passing through rotor and stator one after the other) direct current traction motor.

Resistances are built into the circuit of the motors, which act to cut the voltage for starting purposes. Electric current switched on to traction motors directly at full voltage would be very likely to burn out the electromagnet windings. The

9

resistances are then taken out of the circuit as the speed increases to work at full voltage.

The motor will run at maximum efficiency at its most usual revolution rate.

Most of the engines built as electric or diesel-electric locomotives employed weak-field working, when voltage is reduced to the stator by putting a few parallel-wired resistances into the stator circuit, thereby diverting part of the current into the resistances, causing the voltage to drop. Up to five resistances are used, and these usually correspond to notches on the driver's controller. However as with the very early electrics, today's locomotives are not designed for weak-field working, having instead a solid-state separately-controlled supply to both rotor and stator so as to match efficiency, and this provides maximum efficiency throughout, no matter what the revolution rate.

Although Werner Siemens' locomotive had been the first electric train to run in 1879, progress was initially rapid after that. Thomas Edison ran a trial locomotive in 1880 in the United States, fed with current from a running rail. Stephen Field was the first to take out a patent on

The world's first electric train carries a load of 18 passengers on 31 May 1879, at the Berlin Trades Fair

a similar system, and together with Edison founded the Electric Railway Company of America in 1883, the direct descendant of which is the General Electric Corporation of the United States. Siemens went on to build a 2.5km (1.5-mile) long tramway in a Berlin suburb in 1881, which used a 100V current taken from the running rails. This was followed by a similar tramway in

Siemens Original B

Country of origin: Germany
Railway: Berlin Trades Fair
Date: 1879
Type: demonstration electric locomotive
Gauge: 450mm (1ft 5.75in)
Length overall: 1.57m (5ft 2in)
Propulsion: 150V direct current fed via a raised centre conductor rail and liquid control resistance to a 3.75kW (5hp) motor, which was connected by gearing to the driving wheels
Maximum axle load: not known, but 30 passengers were carried back to back on three carriages
Maximum speed: 13km/h (8mph)
History: the first successful use of electric power for a train, Werner von Siemens' locomotive ran on a circular track of about 0.4km (0.25 mile). Direct current was suppled by a small steam-driven power station and the loco (still on exhibition in the Deutsches Museum, München, Germany) was started and controlled by a liquid resistance. The current was collected by a central third rail, and the return path was via the wheels and running rails.

Paris. The street tramways used two overhead conductors, not being able to use a third rail owing to street *débris* and the mud and wet which made insulation difficult. In some instances, the tramcar towed a little trolley which ran on the overhead track, giving rise to the term trolleycar in the USA. The current was delivered from the trolley to the tramcar motors by way of a cable. Perhaps the most successful of these early direct current electrics is Volk's Electric Railway, which runs along Brighton Pier, opened in 1883; it is still operating.

THREE-PHASE ELECTRIFICATION

Towards the end of the nineteenth century, there was a great deal of development in electrification, as alternating current with three-wire (each wire being known as a phase) transmission proved to be the most economical method. The wires ran from the generators and it is the rate of revolution of a generator which determines the number of reversals of current output per second. These cycles or units of frequency are referred to as Hertz (Hz) after the German physicist Heinrich Hertz, who first showed that radio waves have common characteristics with electromagnetic wave motions such as light.

Most commonly throughout the world, industrial-frequency electricity is generated at a standard 50Hz; however, in North America, Japan and in some parts of South America, 60Hz is the standard.

The problem with these high industrial frequencies is that the three-phase motors revolve too fast for railway use, and thus early three-phase electrification was limited to those minor railways where high power was not necessary. The first three-phase electrification

He 2/2 Nos 1-4

Country of origin: Switzerland
Railway: Gornergrat Railway (GGB)
Date: 1898
Type: rack and pinion railway locomotive
Gauge: 1m (3ft 3.4in)
Length overall: 4.13m (13ft 6.5in)
Total weight: 11.5 tonnes (25,365lb)
Propulsion: 40Hz (550V) three-phase current fed via two conductors and the running rails to two 68kW (90hp) motors, which were geared to the driving pinions
Tractive effort: 78kN (17,632lb)
Maximum speed: 8km (5mph)
History: mountain railways

A Gornergrat Railway He 2/2

was in 1896, of the Lugano tramway; this was followed in 1899 by the electrification of the narrow-gauge railways up the Jungfrau and Gornergrat mountains in Switzerland. In each instance, 40Hz was used, but since then $16\frac{2}{3}$Hz frequency has been used successfully in Switzerland. This enables the traction motors to run at a speed that enables the rotors to be coupled directly to the locomotive driving wheels.

Italy was the only major State railway fully to utilise three-phase electrification.

One major drawback of the three-phase system was the constant speed of the locomotive. Italian freight trains could only run at two speeds, 25 and 50km/h (15.5 and 31mph), and Italian passenger locomotives at four speeds, 37.5, 50, 75 and 100km/h (23.25, 31, 46.5 and 62mph). In addition to this, the $16\frac{2}{3}$Hz current was insufficient to provide lighting, therefore the locomotives had to carry acetylene headlamps. Supply was provided via two overhead wires and from an earthed running rail, each representing a phase. Italian three-phase working finished in 1976, and is now almost completely extinct elsewhere.

SINGLE-PHASE ELECTRIFICATION

By reducing one of the three-phase overhead wires, a much higher operating voltage can be used, as there are far fewer insulation problems for two wires in parallel. This is done by connecting an electrical load across two of the transformer's phase output wires. This leaves two wires, of which one is neutral, and single-phase alternating current is obtained from balancing the three-phase input by a further separate connection between the remaining wire and the neutral phase.

Although this sounds very simple, the single-phase traction motor is very complex and the first single-phase 25Hz railway did not appear until 1905 in the USA, and only in 1903 in Europe, when a stretch of the former Royal Prussian Union Railway's Niederschönweide to Spindlersfelde line was equipped by AEG, using an induction type traction motor known as the Winter-Eichberg type. The 25Hz single-phase system disappeared from Europe in 1908, being replaced by $16\frac{2}{3}$Hz at 15,000V, which is today's standard in Germany, Austria, Switzerland, Norway and Sweden.

Some thirty years later, in

The Class Ae 4/4 introduced the concept of 1,000hp per axle in 1944

Class Ae 4/4 Bo-B

Railway: Berne-Lötschberg-Simplon Railway (BLS)
Date: 1944
Type: electric mixed-traffic mountain locomotive
Gauge: 1.435m (4ft 8.5in)
Length overall: 15.6m (51ft 2in)
Total weight: 80 tonnes (176,320lb)
Propulsion: 16.66Hz (15,000V) single-phase low-frequency alternating current, fed via overhead catenary
Maximum axle load: 20 tonnes (44,080lb)
Tractive effort: 236kN (52,900lb)
Maximum speed: 125km/h (78mph)

1933, Hungarian State Railways electrified the Budapest to Hegyeshalom by line, utilising single-phase 50Hz 15,000V alternating current. Designed by Kálmán Kando, the locos carried a phase converter in the form of an alternating-current single-phase electric motor which ran together with a three-phase generator. In turn this produced an output of three, four and six-phase current. The driving wheels were coupled with the rotor of a single large induction traction motor, and running speeds of 25, 50, 75 and 100km/h (15.5, 31, 46.5 and 62mph) were produced.

This was the first use of industrial-frequency electricity, and it proved to be cheaper than low-frequency single-phase, but more costly than the high voltage direct current.

In 1951, France produced the first workable single-phase industrial-frequency locomotive, since when it has proved to be the cheapest form of railway electrification, the current being carried in an overhead contact wire with 25,000V being set as the highest safe voltage except in open unpopulated areas, where 50,000V has been used.

During the 1950s, a sturdy mercury-arc rectifier had been perfected in the USA, and when this was fitted into a locomotive the line voltage could be reduced. British Rail first mounted an electric solid-state rectifier into a trial motor coach in 1955, and today solid-state rectifiers are the norm, and the mercury-arc type no longer used.

The solid-state thyristor was invented in the USA in 1957, and has become standard as a method by which the train's driver can control current they supply to the traction motors, arranged in a circuit so that their output is all in the same direction. The thyristors also act as a rectifier, and may be known as choppers when employed to control direct current motive power, acting to chop the current into bursts. First used by Netherlands Railways, the chopper form of motive power has been slower to spread than the thyristor-controlled system.

The Class 120 Bo-Bo below incorporated the advanced thyristor-controlled electric circuits outlined overleaf

Class 120 Bo-Bo

Railway: German Federal
Railway (DB)
Date: 1979
Type: mixed-traffic electric
locomotive
Gauge: 1.435m (4ft 8.5in)
Length overall: 19.2m (63ft)
Total weight: 84 tonnes
(185,140lb)
Propulsion: 16.66Hz (15,000V)
alternating current, fed from
overhead catenary rectified by
thyristors and then inverted
by thyristors to variable-
frequency three-phase ac for
supply to four 1,400kW
(1,880hp) induction traction
motors with spring drive
Maximum axle load: 21 tonnes
(46,280lb)
Tractive effort: 340kN (76,440lb)
Maximum speed: 160km/h
(100mph)
History: the development of
thyristors opened up a totally
new future for the induction
motor, having the ability to
switch the current on and off
very quickly and very
precisely. They can be used to
'invert' dc to ac by
interrupting a dc current, and
by inverting three circuits
with an interval of one-third of
a 'cycle' between each, a three-
phase ac supply can be
produced and varied within
wide limits.

CURRENT-INVERTER LOCOMOTIVES

Brown Boveri in Germany
made the traction current-
inverter breakthrough in 1971.

It was not until 1985, however,
that the USA saw its first current inverter locomotive, by
which time there were 450 diesels or electrics running in
Europe. The first European
locomotive was a German Federal Railways 1.86Mw (2,500hp)
Co-Co diesel, No 202 002-2. The
first North American version
was a rebuilt standard 2.24Mw
(3,000hp) diesel, and a multiple-
unit electric train (emu) was
commissioned for the New York
City subway.

All early current-inverter
locomotives used the induction
three-phase traction motor.

A diesel engine and alternator will produce three-phase
current which is solid-state
rectified to direct current; an
electric locomotive can take
direct current from the overhead contact wire otherwise it
is able to rectify an alternating
current supplied on board. The
direct current is presented to a
solid-state inverter, which has
a variable-frequency three-
phase output for traction
motors.

The current inverter is comprised of thyristor switches in

three banks, each bank representing one phase of the three-phase output, which can total as many as are required for the duty of the locomotive. The effect of these switches is to make the current flow first in one direction and then in the other. The switches are controlled simply by the driver. The inverter is able to produce variable current output ranging from as little as 0.5Hz up to 165Hz, and subject to the gearing between the traction motor's rotor and the driving axle, the train's speed varies with the output.

An alternative three-phase motor is the SYnchronous BI-Current (Sybic) developed by French National Railways (SNCF), which converted a B-B monomotor bogie 25,000V single-phase 50Hz locomotive in 1981 to take the long rotor necessary for the Sybic, housed laterally between the body walls.

The Sybic starting circuitry is so arranged that the stator takes moderate frequency three-phase current from the inverter. This is opposed by the rotor, taking direct current supplied through simple slip-rings. The direct current bypasses the inverter. Control is by chopper for the motor's acceleration.

Type BB 26000

Country of origin: France
Railway: French National Railways (SNCF)
Date: 1992
Type: Sybic
Gauge: 1,435mm (54.56in)
Length overall: 17.71m (58ft 1.32in); height 4.27m (14ft 0.12in)
Total weight: 90 tonnes (201,600lb)
Propulsion: 50Hz (25,000V) or 1,500V dc current fed via overhead catenary to a step-down transformer and two rectifier mixed bridges connected in parallel with self-commutating synchronous motor transmission
Tractive effort: 320kW (428.8hp)
Maximum speed: 200km/h (125mph)
History: a self-supporting body type, built in stainless steel, with a protecting shield at each end in front of the driving cab which absorbs energy in the event of a crash, is just part of the application of the newest techniques and technologies employed to create the most efficient general-purpose locomotive in service, enabling the hauling of a 750-tonne (1.68 million lb) passenger train (16 coaches) up a 2.5% gradient at 200km/h (125mph).

SNCF's first of class No 26001 electric Sybic locomotive as seen in 1988 while undergoing trials. The Sybic entered service in 1992

and employs the newest techniques and technologies to *create the most efficient general-purpose locomotive in service*

DIESEL

The world's first diesel-electric unit made its *début* in 1912 in Sweden, when Allmänna Svenska Aktiebolaget (ASEA) converted a 1-A railcar for the Södermanland Midland Railway. It was another 12 years before a 224kW (300hp) Bo-Bo shunting locomotive became the first North American diesel-electric, being built by General Electric of the USA.

Control of the diesel locomotive is usually by the engine revolutions and the demands on the direct current generator are sensed by means of an electromechanical device that increases or decreases the engine's revolutions to meet the demand.

The power is run through all the traction motors, one after the other in series, and the motors themselves are able to act as resistances to cut the voltage for starting.

The diversity of today's diesel engines is enormous, ranging up to more than 447Mw (6,000hp) and diesel current-inverter locomotives compete with the diesel alternator for a future just as current-invertor electrics compete with both thyristor and chopper locomotives.

WHEEL NOTATION

Diesel and electric locomotives are denoted by the number of axles. Letters are given to the driving axles (A = 1, B = 2, C = 3, D = 4) and numbers given to the carrying axles. Independently-powered axles are denoted by an 'o' following the letter. A plus sign accompanying bogie locomotives indicates that traction stresses are transmitted through an articulated member which connects the bogies, rather than via the frame. Power transmission is shown here by black open circles and the carrying axles are shown in blue.

The first main-line diesel units in North America were produced by the Canadian Locomotive Company and Westinghouse Electric in 1929, with 992kW (1,330hp) four-stroke V12 Beardmore diesel engines and generators

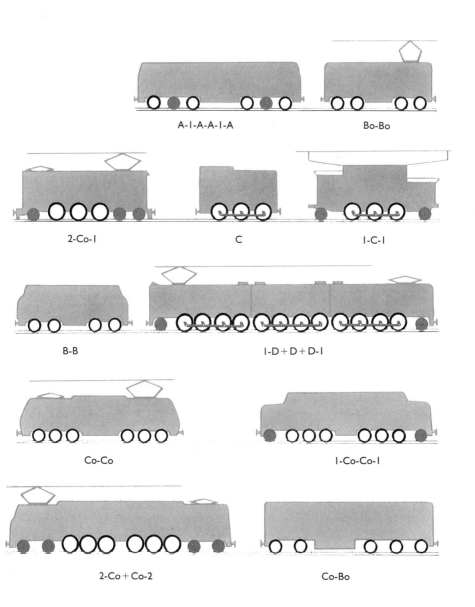

A-1-A-A-1-A

Bo-Bo

2-Co-1

C

1-C-1

B-B

1-D+D+D-1

Co-Co

1-Co-Co-1

2-Co+Co-2

Co-Bo

1 Assistant's Locker
2 Handbrake
3 Twin jet windscreen
   washer
4 Sun visor
5 Horn valve
6 Master controller
7 Cab light switch –
   assistant's
8 Cab light switch – driver's
9 Instrument light switch
10 Control panel air
   conditioning
11 Line voltmeter
12 No.1 and 4 motor ammeter
13 Fault lights – test button
14 Speedometer
15 Windscreen wiper
16 Duplex pressure gauge
17 Off track radio shelf
18 Duplex pressure gauge
19 Duplex vacuum gauge
20 Brake pipe flow indicator
21 Independent brake valve
   D.F.2
22 Tail light switch (No.1 end)
23 Headlight switch (No.2
   end)

24 Tail light switch (No.1 end)
25 Vigilance push button
26 Indicator light – line
27 Indicator light – vigilance
   trip
28 Indicator light – fault
29 Indicator light – wheelslip
30 Push button – V.C.B. open
31 Push button – V.C.B.
   close/reset
32 Push button – pantograph
   up
33 Push button – pantograph
   down
34 Windscreen – intermittent
   wipe – control valve
35 Wiper control valve
36 Washer control valve
37 Release valve – WTV 8/1
38 Brake valve – D14A
39 Headlight switch (No.1
   end)
40 Sanding switch
41 Vigilance pedal
42 Horn valve
43 Drivers drop table
44 End door

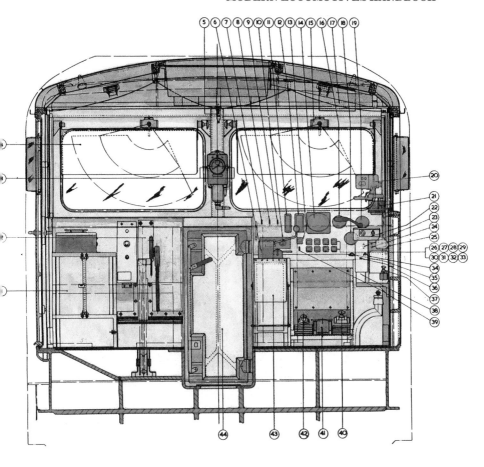

Dimensions

Gauge: 1.065m (41.54in)
Length over buffer beams:
20.120m (65ft 4.7in)
Height: (pantograph down)
3.9m (12ft 8in)
Width: 2.9m (9ft 5in)
Bogie wheelbase: 3.94m (12ft
9.66in)
Pivot centres 12.7m (41ft 3.3in)

*Cab arrangement for a GEC
Alsthom 50kV thyristor-
controlled heavy freight
locomotive with Co-Co wheel
arrangement*

23

RAILWAY SYSTEMS

Albanian Railways (HRPS Sh)
Gauge: 1,435mm (54.56in)
Extent: 338km (209.9 miles)
A predominantly mountainous country with 70% of the territory at elevations of more than 328m (1,000ft), its transport system is State-owned, with rail handling 46% of all freight and 36% passenger traffic.

Algerian National Railways (SNTF)
Gauge: 1,432 and 1,055mm (56.42 and 41.57in)
Extent: 2,649 and 1,112km (1,645 and 690 miles)
Electrification: 296km (183.82 miles) at 3kV dc
The basic network comprises two standard-gauge coastal lines running east 370km (229.77 miles) and west 550km (341.55 miles) from Algiers. The 520km (322.92 miles) north-south line connects east of Algiers.

The 1,432mm (56.42in) gauge operates with 25 electric and 170 diesel locomotives, and 32 twin-unit diesel railcars, compared with the 38 diesel locomotives of the narrow gauge.

Argentine Railways (FA)
Gauge: 1,000, 1,435 and 1,676mm (39.4, 56.54 and 66.03in)
Extent: 34,172km (21,220.81 miles)

Electrification: 196km (121.72 miles) at 600V and 800V dc, plus 40km (24.84 miles) at 25kV 50Hz.
Until the turn of the century, Argentina had one of the world's most efficient railway networks, which by 1913 made it the third largest exporter in the world, but today the equipment is obsolete. The railways that had opened up South Africa and India and expanded had repeated the act in Argentina, using imported drivers, firemen and managers, mainly from the UK. Moreover the railways made a profit, albeit for their British-owned parent companies, which had selfishly British-built stations, bridges and rail and rolling stock. Also too, they burned British coal. In 1946, General Peron came to power and nationalised the railways. Argentina purchased the assets and from that moment onwards everything went wrong. The railways started to disintegrate through lack of investment, rolling stock was left to rust, and while roads were built the railways fell into desuetude, along with the Argentinean economy. By 1989, when the new Menin Government returned the railways to the private sector, 45% of the fleet and 50% of the network had disappeared.

AUSTRALIA

Australian National Railways (ANR)

Gauge: 1,435, 1,067 and 1,600mm (56.54, 42.04 and 63.04in)

Extent: 3,636, 1,813km (including Tasmania's 851km/ 526.47 miles) and 2,001km (2,257.96, 1,125.87 and 1,242 miles) respectively

By the end of 1986, ANR appeared to have stemmed the steady decline in passenger business which had resulted from competition from both air and coach operators, while the freight forwarding in containers and covered wagons provided the bulk of ANR's income. At that time, 262 locomotives were employed, of which 100 were scheduled to be replaced. Initial replacement started with 12 class DL 2,238kW (3,000hp) units in 1988.

Above: *ANR's EL Class Co-Co locomotive is used to haul the Indian Pacific and the legendary Ghan passenger trains. The 2,460kW engine is capable of a maximum speed of 140km/h (86.94mph)*

Below: *the upgraded XPT3, which is based on Britain's HST 125, and was successfully adapted to Australian conditions in 1981*

State Railway Authority (SRA), New South Wales

Gauge: 1,435mm (56.54in)
Extent: 9,908km (6,152.87 miles)
Electrification: 566km (351.486 miles) at 1.5kV dc overhead

The XPT made its *début* in 1981, and today is Australia's fastest train. It has helped SRA to improve its financial standing, adding considerably to its passenger traffic. This had started at 218.6 million journeys in 1986, when its locomotives totalled 98 electrics and 593 diesels, plus double-deck suburban and inter-urban and single-deck inter-urban cars, plus the XPTs and other diesel railcars/multiple units.

XPT eight-car train

Country of origin Australia
Railway: Countrylink
Date: 1981
Type: diesel hydraulic high-speed passenger train
Gauge: 1,435mm (54.56in)
Length overall: 17.3m (56ft 9.12in) driving car
Total weight: 71.13 tonnes (156,800lb) driving car
Propulsion: one 1,492kW (2,000hp) turbocharged two-stroke Paxman Valenta 12-cylinder diesel electric engine hp)
Maximum speed: 193km/h (119.85mph)

Queensland Railways' diesel-electric 98-tonne (215,050 lb) Class 2130 Co-Cos entered service in 1970

Queensland Government Railways

Gauge: 1,435mm (56.54in) interstate line; 1,067mm (42.04in)
Extent: 773 and 10,114km (480 and 6,280.79 miles) respectively
Electrification: 492km (305.53 miles) of 1,067mm (42.04in) gauge at 25kV 50Hz ac

The State-owned Queensland Railways is the second largest in route-km in the British Commonwealth, and serves the whole of the north-eastern part of Australia. The 1,435mm (56.54in) interstate line connects Brisbane with Sydney via the coastal route.

Electric emu railcars number 88, electric Bo-Bo-Bo locomotives 6, diesel locomotives 655 and there are 23 railcars.

South Australia State Transport Authority

Gauge: 1,600mm (63.04in)
Extent: 152.8km (94.89 miles)
Electrification: Since 1978, the Authority has only controlled the metropolitan railway of Adelaide, which is integrated with both the bus and tram services in the city.

26

Victoria State Transport Authority (V/Line)

Gauge: 1,600 and 1,435mm (63.04 and 56.54in)
Extent: 5,448 and 332km (3,383.21 and 206.17 miles)
Electrification: 417km at 1.5kV dc

Aggressive marketing during the 1980s has turned round the gradual diminution of passengers in interstate travel, and new stock is being added to the 25 electric locomotives and the 279 diesel-electrics, most of which had been Clyde-GM built. On the freight traffic side, 25% (3 million tonnes/6,613 million lb) of the annual tonnage is accounted for by grain. The system links Melbourne with Sydney and Adelaide via the interstate trunk route.

Above: *The 25 N Class*
Below: *the G Class locomotives*

Western Australian Government Railways (Westrail)

Gauge: 1,067mm, 1,435mm (42.03, 56.54in) and dual-gauge
Extent: 4,169, 1,212 and 172km (2,589, 752.65 and 106.8 miles)
Responsible for all Western Australian railways running throughout the State, with the sole exception of the Trans-Australian line and some iron ore railways in the northern region, it carries 6 million tonnes/year (13,227.6 million lb).

Austrian Federal Railways (ÖBB)

Gauge: 1,435, 1,000 and 760mm (56.54, 39.4 and 29.94in)
Extent: 5,393, 15.5 and 363km (3,349.05, 9.63 and 225.42 miles) respectively
Electrification: 1,435mm (56.54in) gauge 3,040km (1,887.84 miles) at 15kV 16$\frac{2}{3}$Hz ac; 1,000mm (39.4in) gauge 2.2km (1.37 miles) at 3kV dc and 760mm (29.94in) gauge 91km (56.51 miles) at 6.5kV 25Hz ac
The complexity of the problems posed by a small, mountainous country has never stopped ÖBB from maintaining a high degree of investment in both rolling stock and infrastructure, and today's railroad continues to explore co-operative projects with its neighbours, following the extensive S-Bahn developments during the 1980s.

Class 1044 Bo-Bo

Country of origin: Austria
Railway: Austrian Federal Railways (ÖBB)
Date: 1974
Type: electric express passenger loco
Gauge: 1,435mm (54.56in)
Length overall: 16m (52ft 6in)
Total weight: 84 tonnes (185,140lb)
Propulsion: 16$\frac{2}{3}$Hz (15,000V) low-frequency alternating current fed via overhead catenary with step-down transformer with thyristor control system to four 1,317kW (1,765hp) traction motors driving the axles through Brown Boveri spring drives and gearing
Maximum axle load: 21 tonnes (46,285lb)
Tractive effort: 314kN (70,600lb)
Maximum speed: 160km/h (100mph)
History: two prototypes were produced by the State-owned locomotive building firm of Simmering-Graz-Pauker in 1974, and these were followed by an order for 96 designed specifically for the surefootedness necessary for the mountainous Austrian system and not for speed. They featured the stepless thyristor control, among other developments, that produced exceptional adhesion values.

Above: ÖBB's Class 1044 rostered to haul 550 tonnes (1,212,750lb) up 3.076% (1 in 32.5) ascents

Below: Austria's Class 1020 originally German Class E94 from 1941

Bangladesh Railway Board (BRB)

Gauge: 1,676 and 1,000mm (66.03 and 39.4in)
Extent: 979 and 1,913km (607.96 and 1,187.97 miles) respectively
Since 1982, the system has been under the Director-General's control. The network has been split into two administrative areas; the western area is basically broad gauge and the larger metre-gauge network is in the east.

BELGIUM

Société Nationale des Chemins de fer Belges (SNCB)

Gauge: 1,435mm (56.54in)
Extent: 3,667km (2,277.21 miles)
Electrification: 2,450km (1,521 miles) at 3kV dc
The key Antwerpen-Bruxelles route has recently been upgraded, with complete track renewal to permit greater speeds, together with the re-signalling to allow reversible working. The high-speed line from Paris is scheduled to connect through to Köln, while another line is planned to connect Bruxelles to the Channel Tunnel at Calais. At present, maximum speeds are 140km/h (86.94mph) on major lines and 120km/h (74.52mph) on all other main lines.

Bolivian National Railways (FNFE)

Gauge: 1,000mm (39.4in)
Extent: 3,642km (2,261.68 miles)
The railways play an important role in the Bolivian economy. With funds from the World Bank and others, they have been able to upgrade some lines. Others have been extended to link up with tin mines and soya bean industries while an electrification scheme is in hand.

BRAZIL

Rede Ferroviaria Federal SA (RFFSA)

Gauge: 1,600, 1,000 and 762mm (63.04, 39.4 and 30.02in)
Extent: 1,859, 20,965 and 13km (1,154.44, 13,019.27 and 8.07 miles) respectively
Electrification: 483km (299.94 miles) at 3kV dc
Basically a freight operator with less than 1% of its revenue coming from passenger business, and over half of the annual 100 million tonnes (220,460 million lb) of freight comprising iron ore, coal, and petroleum (gasoline).

Companhia Brasileira de Trens Urbanes (CBTU)

Gauge: 1,600 and 1,000mm (63.04 and 39.4in)
Extent: 776 and 205km (481.89

and 127.31 miles) respectively
Electrification: 776km (481.9
miles) at 3kV dc
Over one million passengers
travel daily on the 1,500 train
services offered by CBTU's fleet
of over 100 diesels and 550 emu
trainsets.

Ferrovia Paulista SA (FEPASA)
Gauge: 1,600mm, 1,000mm
(63.04, 39.4in) and mixed
1,600mm and 1,000mm
Extent: 1,590, 3,408 and 74km
(987.39, 2,116.37 and 45.95 miles)
respectively
Electrification: 1,532km (951.37
miles) at 3kV dc
An amalgamation of five railways in 1970, all of which were
owned by the State of São
Paulo. Since then the railway
has abandoned its long-
distance passenger traffic to
concentrate on major commodity freight, including oil and
agricultural produce.

Vitoria a Minas Railway (EVFM)
Gauge: 1,000mm (39.4in)
Extent: 895km (555.8 miles)
Owned since 1977 solely by Com-
panhia Vale do Rio Doce, the
biggest producers in the world
of iron ore. Its trains normally
comprise 160 cars of 100 tonnes
(220,460lb) gross weight, hauled
by two 2,686kW (3,600hp) diesel
locomotives.

Bulgarian State Railways
Gauge: 1,435 and 760mm (5
and 29.94in)
Extent: 4,341 and 245km (2,690.76
and 152.15 miles) respectively
Electrification: 2,050km (1,273.05
miles) at 25kV 50Hz ac
The volume of both freight and
passenger traffic has continued
to grow, together with the electrification of the network. All
of its electric locomotives are
supplied by the Czechoslovak
Škoda works.

Burma Railways Corporation (BRC)
Gauge: 1,000mm (39.4in)
Extent: 3,137km (1,948 miles)
Rolling stock includes about
250 diesels and half as many
steam locomotives.

*A Type M 1200 diesel-hydraulic
B-B of Burma Railways
Corporation*

CAMEROON

Regie Nationale des Chemins de Fer du Cameroun (Regifercem)
Gauge: 1,000mm (39.4in)
Extent: 1,143km (709.8 miles)
Rolling stock includes over 100 diesel locomotives.

CANADA

Algoma Central Railway
Gauge: 1,435mm (56.54in)
Extent: 518km (321.68 miles)
Founded about a hundred years ago; today's rolling stock comprises 31 locomotives, with nine EMD 2,238kW (3,000hp) Type SD-40s.

BC Rail
Gauge: 1,435mm (56.54in)
Extent: 2,846km (1,767.37 miles)
Electrification: 129km (80.11 miles) at 50kV 60Hz
Organised in 1984, this is the operating subsidiary of the British Columbia Railway Company. It operates over 10,000 freight cars, 104 diesel and 7 electric locomotives.

Canadian National (CN Rail)
Gauge: 1,435 and 1,067mm (56.54 and 42.04in)
Extent: 45,571 and 1,142km (28,299.59 and 709.18 miles)
CN serves all ten provinces, and the two northern territories,

providing access to the country's very rich national resources. It has an extensive army of some 1,870 diesel locomotives, including many built in the 1950s, plus 14 electrics, and is responsible for hauling over 80,000 freight cars.

CP Rail

Gauge: 1,435mm (56.54in)
Extent: 23,623km (14,669.88 miles)

In addition to its own track, CP operates on a further 10,000km (6,210 miles) of routes, and the network serves all Canada with the exception of Newfoundland and Prince Edward Island. Its main-line fleet of 1,250 consists largely of General Motors 2,238kW (3,000hp) SD 40-2 diesel-electrics.

Cartier Railway

Gauge: 1,435mm (56.54in)
Extent: 416km (258.34 miles)

Built for the transportation of iron ore, which is worked in trains of 150 cars hauled by three 2,238kW (3,000hp) locomotives used in front during the summer, but in the colder weather one is dropped to the rear. The fleet numbers 48 diesel-electric locomotives.

GO Transit

Gauge: 1,435mm (56.54in)
Extent: 341km (211.76 miles)

Total passenger journeys number about 25 million, carried on a fleet of 32 General Motors of Canada diesel locomotives. Rolling stock also includes over 200 bi-level cars in GO Transit's colourful livery.

Left: *current CP diesel power*   Above: *a GP 40 TC of GO Transit*

Québec North Shore and Labrador Railway
Gauge: 1,435mm (56.54in)
Extent: 638.77km (396.68 miles)
The line was begun in 1950 by the Iron Ore Company of Canada, together with support from several US steelmakers, and runs 57 diesel-electric locomotives.

VIA Rail Canada Ltd
Extent: 21,353km (13,260.21 miles)
VIA Rail became a separate company in 1978, responsible for all of the passenger services previously operated by CN and CP Rail, with the exception of commuter services. In 1986, 290 CN stations and 150 CP stations, together with 1,300 staff and 600 train crews came under VIA control.

CHILE

Chilean State Railways (EFE)
Gauge: 1,676 and 1,000mm (66.03 and 39.4in)
Extent: 4,085 and 30,006km (2,536.79 and 18,633.73 miles) respectively
Electrification: 1,891km (1,174.31 miles) of 1,676mm (66.03in) gauge at 3kV dc
In 1983, the system was decentralised into three separate area railways; FC del Norte, which is basically metre-gauge north of Santiago; FC del Sur, which extends south from Santiago to Puerto Montt and is essentially 1,676mm (66.03in) gauge, much of which is electrified; and the third, FC Arica, which extends from Arica to Visviri, a distance of only 206km (127.93 miles), to link with the Bolivian Railways.

Antofagasta and Bolivian Railway PLC (FLAB)

Gauge: 1,000mm (39.4in)
Extent: 751km (466.37 miles)
Reorganised in 1981, this railway runs from the Pacific at Antofagasta to the Argentinian and Bolivian borders. Traction includes 18 General Motors-built diesels.

Chinese People's Republic Railways (CPRR)

Gauge: 1,435mm (56.54in) with some 750mm (29.55in)
Extent: in excess of 50,000km (31,050 miles)
Electrification: approximately 5,000km (3,105 miles) at 25kV 50Hz ac

In 1986 the Ministry of Railways was made financially autonomous, since when it has extended national manufacture of diesels under licence, including the building of over 1,000 Dong Feng 4 freight Co-Cos of 2,462kW (3,300hp), based on Soviet designs. In addition large orders were placed for Japanese, European and also North American-built diesels. An electrification programme continues, and now includes the line from the Hong Kong border to Beijing.

Left: *VIA tilt-body LRC train crosses the Richelieu River at Beloeil, Québec, east of Montréal*

Below and overleaf: *Bo-Bo + Bo-Bo electric locomotives Type 8K*

35

Type 8K Bo-Bo + Bo-Bo driving cab bottom centre *and side view* bottom left. *The main exploded diagram which shows the propulsion unit is courtesy of GEC Alsthom, whose production line for the Type 8K is illustrated* below right

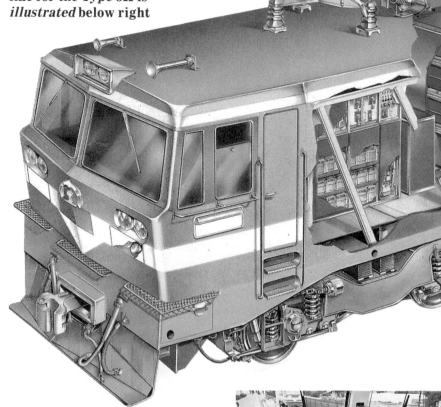

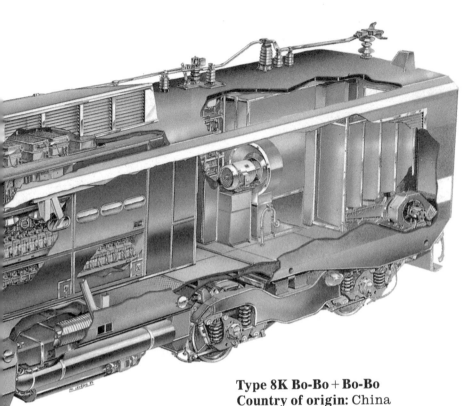

Type 8K Bo-Bo + Bo-Bo
Country of origin: China
Railway: Ministry of Railways
of the People's Republic of
China
Date: 1988
Type: double electric
locomotive for heavy freight
Gauge: 1,435mm (54.56in)
Length overall: 36.228m (118ft
10.32in); height 3.98m (13ft
0.72in)
Total weight: 184 tonnes
(405,646lb)
Propulsion: 50Hz (25,000V) fed
via overhead catenary.
Transmission is by pinion
shrunk on the end of the
motorshaft and driving a gear
wheel on the axle.

National Railways of Columbia (FN de C)
Gauge: 914mm (36.01in)
Extent: 3,246km (2,015.77 miles), not all of which is worked
Much of the system is in poor condition, as is the motive power, which comprises in theory nearly 150 diesel locomotives.

Chemin de Fer Congo-Océan (CFCO)
Gauge: 1,067mm (42.04in)
Extent: 517km (321.06 miles)
Motive power includes over 50 diesel-electric locomotives, plus shunters and railcars.

Ferrocarriles de Costa Rica (FECOSA)
Gauge: 1,067mm (42.04in)
Extent: 700km (434.7 miles)
Electrification: 128km (79.49 miles) at 15kV 20Hz and 132km (81.97 miles) at 25kV 60Hz
The country's two railways were merged as the FECOSA in 1977, the principal traffic for which is bananas, with annual tonnage of about 700,000 tonnes (1,543.2 million lb).

Cuban National Railways (F de C)
Gauge: 1,435mm (56.54in)
Extent: 5,053km (3,137.91 miles)
Electrification: 151km (93.77 miles) at 1.2kV dc
A huge fleet of 450 diesels assembled from around the world hauls much of Cuba's freight transport movements, which comprise sugar and sugar byproducts in the main. Cuba has manufactured its own railcars since 1987.

Czechoslovak State Railways (ČSD)
Gauge: 1,435 and 1,520mm (56.54 and 59.89in) plus some narrow gauge
Extent: 12,884, 102 and 146km (8,000.96, 63.34 and 90.66 miles) respectively
Electrification: 1,307km (811.64 miles) at 25kV 50Hz; 2,218.5km (1,377.69 miles) at 3kV dc and 87km (54.03 miles) at 1.5kV dc respectively
Prior to the division of the country into the Czech and Slovakian Republics, the railway system was already split into four regions, each largely autonomous. With a quarter of the system already electrified, the fleet of 1,341 exclusively Škoda-built electric locomotives was already carrying 70% of all traffic.

Danish State Railways (DSB)
Gauge: 1,435mm (56.54in)
Extent: 2,025km (1,257.53 miles)
Electrification: 142km (88.18 miles) at 1.5kV dc and 900km (558.9 miles) at 25kV 50Hz ac
Main-line electric trains began

Class EA 3000 4,000kW (5,360hp) 25kV ac three-phase electric of Danish State Railways

operating between Copenhagen and Helsingør in March 1986, and now almost half of the system is electrified. Although DSB handles 99% of total freight and 95% of total passenger traffic, 13 smallish private railways exist in Denmark, where DSB is also responsible for ferry services operating ten routes.

State Railways of Ecuador (ENFE)
Gauge: 1,067mm (42.04in)
Extent: 965.5km (599.58 miles)

Motive power includes Alco DL 535B Co-Co and Alsthom 716kW (960hp) B-B-B diesel locomotives

Egyptian Railways (ER)
Gauge: 1,435mm (56.54in)
Extent: 4,321km (2,683.34 miles)
Electrification: 25km (15.53 miles) at 1.5kV ac
Concentrated in the more fertile regions of the Nile delta, Cairo, Alexandria and Port Said, traditionally ER has been a passenger service, but line extensions have enabled it to handle greater volumes of freight, which now includes phosphates in addition to aluminium.

Class Dr13 locomotives, which served VR well, are now giving way to electrification

Class Dr13 C-C

Date: 1963
Type: diesel-electric mixed-traffic locomotive
Gauge: 1.524m (5ft)
Length overall: 18.576m (61ft)
Total weight: 99 tonnes (218,200lb)
Propulsion: two 1,303kW (1,400hp) Tampella-MGO Type V-16 BHSR V16 diesel engines and generators
Maximum axle load: 16.5 tonnes (36,370lb)
Tractive effort: 277kN (62,373lb)

Finnish State Railways (VR)

Gauge: 1,524mm (60.05in)
Extent: 5,877km (3,649.62 miles)
Electrification: 1,663km (1,032.72 miles) at 25kV 50Hz ac
VR has continued through the 1980s to upgrade its system, most of which had been laid a century ago, with continuous welding, enabling higher train speeds to be scheduled.

French National Railways (SNCF)

Gauge: 1,435 and 1,000mm (56.54 and 39.4in)
Extent: 34,750 and 99km (21,579.75 and 61.48 miles)
Electrification: 1,000mm (39.4in) gauge 5,737km (3,562.68 miles) at 1.5kV dc; 6,000km (3,726 miles) at 25kV 50Hz ac; 63km (39.12 miles) at 850V dc; 35km (21.74 miles) at 750V dc; 10km (6.21 miles) at 750V dc (third rail) and 18km (11.19 miles) at 650/700V dc (third rail).
One of the world's leading networks, SNCF received an annual subsidy from the Government of FF 35,000 million for the second half of the 1980s, enabling it to stabilise its finances and to accelerate new route construction up to 200km (124.2 miles) per annum. SNCF was also committed to increase passenger and freight traffic by 1% per year, which meant 49,320 million passenger km (30,672.72

million passenger miles) and some 56,200 million tonnes/km 7,812,180 million lb/mile) by the end of that decade.

Work on the Channel Tunnel began in 1987, with the official opening due in May 1994. TGV locomotives scheduled from London to Paris will provide an important link in the TGV network, which was launched in 1981.

The SNCF fleet is impressive, comprising over 3,000 electric, 2,000 diesel and 1,500 tractor locomotives in addition to over 50 gas-turbine trainsets, 10,000 passenger cars and 200,000 freight wagons, of which some

Above: *Class 15000 B-B express passenger locomotives introduced in 1971 on the Paris-Strasbourg line*

Left: *the 1992 Sybic in action*

75,000 are privately owned.

By the end of the 1980s, dual-voltage 5,600kW Sybic class B-B 26000s had been introduced, together with new main-line diesels. Current electric traction development is now based on the use of three-phase ac synchronous motors, each of which consists of a rotor acting as motor inductor and a stator serving as a motor armature, while thyristors undertake the current distribution in the stator conductor. This system provides increased reliability and efficiency, and reduced maintenance costs.

TGV: the world's fastest fleet

The first TGV entered service on 24 September 1981, between Paris and Lyons, and in its first decade the type carried more than 200 million passengers. Developed jointly between SNCF and GEC Alsthom, it was then the fastest train in the world, with speeds of 260km/h (161.46mph) being reached between Paris and Lyons. In 1983, top speeds were increased to 270km/h (167.67mph), and the journey time compared to pre-TGV trainsets cut by two hours. The Paris-Lyons line was the first new main-line constructed in France since 1928. The network was expanded to include St Etienne, Besançon and Genève, and the new route renamed Paris-Sud-Est line. Lausanne was added in 1984, with some TGVs being equipped to run under the 15kV 16⅔Hz Swiss catenary. The same year, a Lille-Lyons TGV line was added, and a service through to the Swiss capital, Berne, in 1987.

During 1989 and 1990 a second TGV line opened in stages along France's Atlantic coast, and became known as *TGV Atlantique*. It is a Y-shaped route, designed for up to 300km/h (186.3mph), bringing the wine capital of Bordeaux to less than three hours' journey time from Paris. This service now reaches Rochelle, where GEC Alsthom makes the TGV trailer cars.

New lines for the 1990s include Paris-Lille-Bruxelles, also the Channel Tunnel project which has taken six years to build at a cost of £10 billion (US$15 billion), and in 1994 the first section of the Paris bypass route round to the east of the city, known as the TGV interconnection; the Sud-Est line will be extended to Valence. In November 1993, a Franco-Italian agreement was reached for a line linking Lyons to Torino. SNCF's overall plan foresees construction of more than 3,500km (2,173.5 miles) of high-speed lines by the year 2010. Meanwhile, Amsterdam, Köln and Frankfurt will become linked by the second half of the 1990s.

The French Post Office had a small fleet of TGVs built and finished in its distinctive yellow livery, which entered service on the Paris-Lyons route in 1984. Constructed with wide centre doors and no windows, the whole train can carry 60 tonnes (132,276lb) of mail at 270km/h (167.67mph).

Such was SNCF's success with the TGVs – the average load factor by 1991 was 73%, with standard tickets sold at the same price as those for any

Above: *the prototype TGV on early trials*

Below: *the 1989 TGVA twelve-car trainset*

other train, although reservations are compulsory and also supplements levied for peak travel times – that SNCF was able to pay off the entire cost of the Paris-Lyons line, including interest charges, after the first ten years of operation.

The blue/silver grey livery announced the *TGV Atlantique*, the second generation of TGVs which embodied important innovations, increased the maximum speeds when in service, and had ten instead of eight trailer cars, which provide 30% more capacity. The power cars are fitted with self-commutating synchronous traction motors, giving a continuous rating of 4,400kW for each power car, and although more powerful these take up only the same space as the TGV Sud-Est trains, but need less maintenance. In addition, the restyling of the profile gives a 10% gain in aerodynamic performance. The TGV-A also had, for the first time on a high-speed passenger train, an onboard computer network, monitoring the performance and functioning of all the most important equipment, including the brakes, traction gear, drives and cab signalling, plus air conditioning and bogie stability. The driver is able to keep in radio contact with

other TGV trains, central control and with the despatching office at Paris Montparnasse.

Such is the forethought and consideration used in customer care that heating and air-conditioning are programmed to be switched on automatically when preparing a train for departure. Passengers travelling first-class can enjoy at-seat service of meals and are able to select seating in either conventional open salons or in attractive four-seat semi-compartments which offer a 'club' ambiance. A salon in the end trailer has video facilities and can be used for holding business meetings. In second class, a number of seating bays are designed for use by families with children, and seats in a lounge in the end car can be folded back to form a play area.

On 5 December 1989, a TGV-A trainset reduced to a formation of four trailers, and with a gear ratio altered to 4,000rpm at 400 km/h (248.4mph) and upgraded synchronous traction motors giving a total continuous rating of 12,000kW, gained a speed of 482.4km/h (299.57mph). The following May, the very same test train peaked at speeds well in excess of 500km/h (310.5mph). When the formation was reduced to just three trailers and two power cars, combined with aerodynamic improvements which included fairings on the power car roofs and short skirts over the motor bogies, a speed of 515.3km/h (320mph) was reached on 18 May, shattering all previous records for passenger trains.

The Trans-Manche Super-Trains (TMSTs) will be the TGVs of the Channel Tunnel; although quite different from their TGV predecessors, they bear all of their characteristics and will link London to Paris in three hours, as well as running between London and Bruxelles. Of the original fleet order of 38 trainsets, seven are being adapted to run beyond London to the north of England and Scotland. In order to run on the British Rail network, the TMSTs must have a smaller cross-section so that they do not impinge upon the loading gauge; this involved reworking the bodyshell shape and in addition redesigning all of the traction equipment to operate on Belgium's 3kV dc network and with the 750V dc power supply with third rail pick-up as used in southern England.

Maximum speeds in France will be 300km/h (186.3mph), 160km/h (99.36mph) in the Channel Tunnel and 180km/h (111.78mph) in England.

Other TGV descendants

TMSTs under construction

include the AVE trainsets for Spain (*see* Spanish National Railways *page 66*) to operate a new Madrid-Sevila line and a TGV network to link Houston, Texas with Dallas and San Antonio, which is due to open in 1998.

The future of the TGV can only be speculated upon, but GEC Alsthom estimates that by the end of 1995, up to 580 trainsets will be operative and by 2010 up to 1,000. Double-deck designs are planned for the Paris to Lyons and Paris to Bruxelles routes, capable of carrying 45% more passengers, and speeds are earmarked to be increased in commercial service from 300 to 350km/h (217.35mph) through technological advances.

Gabon State Railways (OCTRA)
Gauge: 1,435mm (56.54in)
Extent: 648km (402.41 miles)
Construction on the trans-Gabon route began in 1974, and the first 183km (113.64-mile) section opened in 1979. By 1987, OCTRA operated 22 Alsthom Type BB 100 and ten General Electric UM 22 C diesel main-line locomotives.

GERMANY

Until unification on 1 January 1994, the two systems were as detailed. Fortunately both were standard gauge and used. 15kV 16⅔Hz ac electricity.

German State Railways (DR)
Gauge: 1,435mm (56.54in)
Extent: 13,777km and 277km (8,555.52 and 172.02 miles)
Electrification: 4,500km (2,794.5 miles) at 15kV 16⅔Hz ac
The German Democratic Republic was Europe's second most densely rail-served country, behind Belgium. This was the country's most important transport system, as the Government arranged for most of the nation's freight, about 80%, to be transported by rail. An average of 7,500 daily freight trains ran, in addition to the 7,000 daily passenger trains. By November 1986, DR was hauling 900,000 tonnes (1,984 million lb) daily. Electrification started in 1955, but it was not until 1982 that it was really stepped up, with the objective of electrifying the route from Berlin to the ports of Rostock and Warnemünde, which was completed in 1985. Principal diesel locomotives were VEB-built B-Bs, and USSR Co-Cos, while all major class electrics were supplied by LEW Hennigsdorf.

German Federal Railway (DB)
Gauge: 1,435mm (56.54in)
Extent: 27,778km (17,250.14 miles)
Electrification: 11,395km (7,076.3 miles) at 15kV 16⅔Hz ac
The system was divided into ten regional headquarters, all of which had received backing from the Federal German Transport Plan of 1985, which provided Dm35,000 million in funding for investment until the end of 1995 for more high-speed lines, to be known as Transrapid links. These were primarily to connect the larger cities together, and to the industrial areas badly serviced owing to speed limitations on existing lines. Additionally to these track improvements, links were to be constructed between the cities and the major airports.

In 1986, reorganisation of

regional management elimin-
ated over 100 operating and
mechanical offices and reduced
staffing levels to just over
250,000, approximately half of
the 1958 level.

Passenger traffic on the intercity (IC) network, which was
extended to just over 500km
(310.5 miles) by the end of the
1980s, was increasing at only 1%
per annum despite the introduction of fare incentives in
March 1987.

The City-Bahn concept of
higher-quality suburban services was introduced in 1986
between Köln and Gum-
mersbach, and immediately
increased passenger journeys
on that route by 40%. A grant of
Dm44 million was made by the
Ministry of Research and Technology towards the cost of
building an experimental self-
propelled high-speed trainset,
the Inter-City Experimental
(ICE). The five-car trainset
involved several manufac-
turers and was aimed to test the

Top: *Class E 18, on the right,
entered service in 1935 and
worked until the 1950s*

Centre: *Class 132 about to depart
Berlin station for Dortmund*

Bottom: *Class E 410 German
Federal Railways Bo-Bo*

interaction of various onboard systems at very high speed. The result was a trial in 1986, when a new German record speed of 345km/h (over 214mph) was achieved.

The IC Express subsequently entered production for the launch of services on the München-Wurzburg-Hamburg and the Hamburg-Frankfurt-Stuttgart-München routes, which began in 1991.

With effect from 1 January 1994, the new Deutsche Bahn AG (DBAG) operated as a private undertaking rather than as a nationalised industry, even though the Federal Government was its sole shareholder. The new DBAG operates as 21 regional zones. The services of the old DR still require further modernisation, and a substantial investment programme is underway to improve track, signalling and rolling stock. In

IC Experimental trainset up to 14 cars

Maximum speed: up to 350km/h (217.35mph)
Length overall: 114m (374.03ft)
Seats: first class 60, second class 27
Power car tare weight: 78 tonnes (174,720lb)
Maximum width of car body: 3.07m (10.07ft)

Main picture: *ICE*

Inset: *Class E 120 5,600kW (7,504hp) Bo-Bo electric*

1992, and in 1993, Dm20 billion was injected into the railways. Services will include the high-speed Inter-City Express (ICE) services, which now operate with 100 trains every weekday, including Berlin in the network, and providing for example a service from Frankfurt to Hannover of two hours 22 minutes. Inter-City/Euro-City is based on fast long-distance daytime travel, with a network of nearly 200 trains daily on the interconnecting IC lines which serve leading German centres.

The new Inter-Regio net is designed to provide a high grade service between smaller towns and the larger towns served by the Inter-City system. It comprises 76 lines connecting some 200 stations throughout Germany. In addition to these systems, there is a network of over 20,000 regional and local trains a day, being developed so as to connect the suburbs and outer towns with the major cities and the Regional Bahn (RB) and Regional SchnellBahn (RSB) making convenient connections and linking up with the long-distance network.

Ghana Railway Corporation (GRC)

Gauge: 1,067mm (42.04in)
Extent: 953km (591.81 miles)

A deteriorating network now operating well short of capacity or even financial balance, and of its fleet of approximately 70 locomotives it is unclear how many are serviceable.

GREECE

Hellenic Railways Organisation (CH)

Gauge: 1,435, 1,000 and 750mm (56.54, 39.4 and 29.55in)
Extent: 1,565, 892 and 22km (971.87, 553.93 and 13.66 miles) respectively

The past decade has seen the decline of CH halted and an improved service has attracted both passengers and freight back to the railways, even though it still only attracts 4% of the passenger and 8% of the freight market. Electrification has begun with the 587km (364.53-mile) main line Athens-Thessaloniki-Idomeni at 25kV 50Hz ac. Rolling stock includes over 200 diesel locomotives.

HONG KONG

Kowloon Canton Railway (British section KCR)

Gauge: 1,435mm (56.54in)
Extent: 34km (21.11 miles)
Electrification: 34km (21.11 miles) at 25kV 50Hz ac

Built as early as 1910, the line links Kowloon with the Chinese border at Shum Chun. Responsibility for the running of the Railway was passed from the Government to the Kowloon-Canton Railway Corporation.

Hungarian State Railways (MAV)

Gauge: 1,524, 1,435 and 760mm (60.05, 56.54 and 29.94in)
Extent: 35, 7,405 and 176km (21.74, 4,598.5 and 109.3 miles) respectively
Electrification: 1,920km (1,192.32 miles) at 25kV 50Hz ac

Lines radiate to all sectors of Hungary from Budapest, thus connecting the capital with neighbouring countries. International passenger traffic, especially short-haul, dropped constantly during the 1980s as did freight traffic, for which MAV accounted for about 1% only, but line improvements are gradually being made together with the introduction of new electric and diesel locomotives following MAV's first computer-based signalling control panel which was installed at Miskok in 1986.

Indian Government Railways (IR)

Gauge: 1,676, 1,000, 762, and

610mm (65.36, 39.4, 29.72, and 23.79in)

Extent: 33,669, 23,921 and 4,246km (20,908.45, 14,854.94 and 2,636.77 miles)

Electrification: 1,676mm (66.04in) gauge 6,093km (3,783.75 miles) at 25kV 50Hz ac and 405km (251.5 miles) at 1.5kV dc; 1,000mm (39.4in) gauge 166km (103.09 miles) at 25kV 50Hz ac

Indian Railways is the world's largest State-owned system, and is comprised of nine zonal systems.

Central Railway, initially formed in 1951 with a full mix of the above grades, accounts for about one fifth of all IR's passenger and freight traffic, as it carries about 2.75 million passengers daily between its 678 stations, with the Bombay suburban services accounting for about 80% of total passenger travel.

Eastern Railway, based on Calcutta, is the biggest of the zonal areas and was formed in 1952.

Northern Railway, also created in 1952, extends from Delhi and operates about 250 electric and 450 diesel locomotives, in addition to over 1,000 steam locomotives.

North Eastern Railway is predominantly narrow-gauge, worked mostly by steam. Northeast Frontier Railway,

hived off in 1958 from the North Eastern Railway, serves all of Assam and north Bengal including the famous 610mm (24.03in) gauge Darjeeling to Himalaya Railway, which is still worked by 100-year-old steam trains.

Southern Railway, formed in 1951, is centred on Madras, where most of the line's electrification is to be found. Freight traffic is still expanding and will reach 30 million tonnes (66,138 million lb) a year by the turn of the century, while passenger traffic has fallen. The line boasts a train with the largest itinerary in India, of 3,800km (2,359.8 miles).

South Central Railway was set up in 1966, from sections of both the Southern and Central Railways, and runs about 350 diesels and 950 steam locos.

South Eastern Railway, with just over 7,000km (4,347 miles) of track, was created in 1955, and is based on Calcutta. It handles about one third of all IR's freight traffic, worth some 85% of its revenue.

Western Railways, which was formed in 1951, comprises the former Bombay, Baroda and Central India, Jaipur State, Gaekwar of Baroda's, Cutch State, Saurashtra and Rajasthan Railways and is now IR's biggest passenger carrier.

Indonesian State Railways (PJKA)

Gauge: 1,067mm and 750mm (42.04 and 29.55in)
Extent: 5,914km and 497km (3,672.59 and 308.64 miles)
Electrification: 125km (77.63 miles) at 1.5kV dc

The system is confined to the island of Java, with 4,900km (3,042.9 miles) of track, and Sumatra where the entire 750mm (29.55in) track is to be found. The system was nationalised in the 1950s. In the 1980s, a great deal of upgrading was carried out, including the introduction of many North American-built diesel locomotives, following the demise of the steam locomotives.

Irish Rail

Gauge: 1,602mm (63.12in)
Extent: 1,940km (1,204.74 miles)
Electrification: 38km (23.6 miles) at 1.5kV dc

Iarnród Éireann (Irish Rail) came into being on 2 February 1987, at a time when freight traffic was falling, but passenger traffic showing slight improvement. Rolling stock included 130 diesel locomotives, plus 40 electric multiple units (emus).

Israel State Railways (ISR)

Gauge: 1,435mm (56.54in)
Extent: 520km (323 miles)

From 1985 passenger services have been subsidised to 30% of their cost, but there is no subsidy for freight. The track is entirely single-line, and only 230km (142.83 miles) is operated by passenger trains. Railways account for only 5% of passenger traffic, which is better served by the 10,000km (6,210-mile) bus network.

Italian Railways (FS)

Gauge: 1,435mm (56.54in) and (Sicily) 950mm (37.43in)
Extent: 16,066km and 71km (9,976.99 and 44.09 miles) respectively
Electrification: 8,842km (5,490.88 miles) at 3kV dc

With effect from 1 January 1986, FS became a State corporation. The Government did, however, retain control of internal passenger fares, which remain the lowest in Western Europe. From 1987, an eight-year plan was embarked upon to upgrade the main city traffic hubs, double-tracking of busy routes, upgrading of the main Roma-Napoli line and in addition to many others, electrification, intermodal development, telecommunications and level crossing suppression. In addi-

The ETR 450 began service on the Roma-Napoli link in May 1988

ETR 450

Country of origin: Italy
Railway: Italian State Railways (FS)
Date: 1988
Type: tilting-body high-speed electric passenger train
Gauge: 1,435mm (54.56in)
Length overall: 183.6m (602ft 4.68in)
Total weight: 400 tonnes (896,000lb)
Propulsion: 3,000V dc supplied via overhead catenary with thyristors and diodes for the traction motor shunt system. Series-excited four-pole self-ventilating motors with compensator and auxiliary poles and motor-driven alternator units provide power for auxiliaries. Each train has two traction motors, one per bogie, actuated by two single-phase choppers and controlled by an electric system.
Maximum axle load: 12.5 tonnes (28,000lb)
Tractive effort: 192kN (43,200lb)
Maximum speed: 250km/h (155.25mph)
History: the ETR 450 began service on the Roma-Milano link in May 1988, running to a scheduled time of 3hrs 58min, and on the Roma-Venezia route at the end of 1989. It comprises eight powered vehicles, plus a trailer.

tion, a huge effort has been made to improve international routes. New timetables introduced in 1987 dropped the TEE category of intercity services, and the ETR 450 tilt-body trainsets that were introduced on the main Roma-Milano route initially cut journey time by 40 minutes, which was further reduced as line improvements permitted speeds of up to 250km/h (155.25mph) on the *Direttissima*. The ETR 450s are first-class only, with each salon seating 45. They were followed into production by the ETR 500, a non tilt-body trainset also developed by Fiat Ferroviaria Savigliano, but with mechanical assistance from Breda. The latter is also responsible for the car body and interior design. The ETR 500 has a 300km/h (186.3mph) capability.

The principle underlying the tilting-body system, which allows the train to lean into the curves, is the same as that used in railway line construction, when tracks are canted around bends. The idea is to compensate for part of the centrifugal acceleration in proportion to the vehicle's speed and the sweep of the curve. Tilting the body on winding routes produces a virtual body cant which, together with lower axle weight, makes for improved

ride comfort, higher speed around curves and less track wear. The Fiat Ferroviaria-built ETR 450 *Pendolino* was designed with these criteria in mind. The ETR 450 is an important achievement and was the result of 20 years of research into wheel/rail interaction.

The world's first tilting-body train was the prototype ETR 401 of 1976 (*illustrated above*); 130 tilting-body units designed for use in nine-unit trainsets have been supplied to FS since 1985, and are now scheduled on the 600km (372.6-mile) Roma-Milano service in less than four hours. The ETR 450 is also employed on the Milano-Torino, the Roma-Napoli and Roma-Venezia lines.

Both computer-aided design and computer-aided production were employed by Fiat to produce a unit that comprises a

The Fiat Ferroviaria-built ETR 401 **Pendolino** *four-car trainset*

unitary body constructed of large light alloy sections. Each body is supported on two bogies, and carries two traction motors suspended lengthwise under the floor. Each motor actuates the bogie's internal axle through a U-joint drive shaft and a bevel gear final drive. Body-bogie connection is provided through an auxiliary bolster beam. Vertical and transverse suspension is provided by flexicoil spring sets, while the active lateral suspension system improves the ride comfort by helping reduce transverse acceleration.

The body is sprung from the bolster beam through link rods and is tilted in curves by paired electronically-controlled hydraulic cylinders.

IVORY COAST

Regie des Chemins de Fer Abidjan-Niger (RAN)

Gauge: 1,000mm (39.4in)
Extent: 549km (340.93 miles)
With traffic constantly falling throughout the 1980s, RAN was still able to operate its 47 main-line diesel-electric locomotives, which included 19 General Motors (GM) 1,679kW (2,250hp) Co-Cos and six General Motors of Canada 1,679kW (2,250hp) Class GT 22 LC.

Japan Railways Group (JR)

Gauge: 1,067mm in 1987; Shinkansen 1,435mm (56.54in)
Extent: 20,789km (12,909 miles) in 1987; 5,775km (3,586.28 miles) double or multi-track
Electrification: 5,493km (3,411.15 miles) at 1.5kV dc, 2,173km (1,349 miles) at 20kV 50Hz ac, 1,372km (852.01 miles) at 20kV 60Hz ac; Shinkansen 1,177km (730.92 miles) at 25kV 60Hz ac (Tokaido, Sanyo), 835km (518 miles) at 25kV 50Hz ac (Joetsu, Tokoku)
In 1854 the locomotive was introduced to Japan. It was quickly accepted; by the turn of the century Japan had its own locomotive industry, providing it with what the Japanese considered the ideal transport system, which was meticulously controlled from the outset. With no military expenditure to consider following the Second World War, Japan continued to invest heavily in the railways, and in 1964 the Shinkansen line opened.

Although the railways still did not pay their way, Japan National Railways (JNR) forged ahead, still expanding the system with Government money. It also invested in new technology, so that by 1987 its losses were 10% of Japan's GNP, about £2,000 (US$3,500) per person in the country.

Something had to happen, and in April 1987 JNR was statutorily ended and its assets, operations and liabilities were distributed among a number of new companies which became known as the Japan Railways Group. The railways had first been nationalised in the 1920s, but this still allowed for some private railways to exist and these had grown up with the communities they served, operating supermarkets, land and even funeral parlours. They identified themselves with their customers and thrived, so that by 1987 there were more private railway companies in Japan than in any other country.

The train is ideal for crowded cities, and for moving large numbers of people, provided

that every part of the system operates like clockwork; thus a train is able to depart Tokyo every 3.5 minutes. Japan invested heavily in its rail system, with scant regard for cost. This means that it now transports about 90% of those working in Tokyo, 38 million passengers each day and still growing.

Japan's is the envy of the world's railways; fast, clean, highly organised and integrated across a wide range of requirements.

The break up of JNR and the launching of the new companies on the stock market does not, however, mean that the Government will not continue to back them in the future or to come to their aid if necessary.

East Japan Railway Company
Extent: 7,454km (4,628.93 miles)
Based on Tokyo metropolitan area, it includes responsibility for the Tokoku and Joetsu Shinkansen.

A Bullet Train line-up

West Japan Railway Company
Extent: 5,091km (3,161.51 miles)
Osaka is the centre for this company, which has responsibility for the Sanyo Shinkansen.

Hokkaido Railway Company
Extent: 2,542km (1,578.58 miles)
A passenger traffic railway based in Sapporo.

Kyushu Railway Company
Extent: 2,101km (1,304.72 miles)
Responsible for the region, Kyushu is based in Fukuoka.

Shikoku Railway Company
Extent: 837km (519.78 miles)

All freight is handled by Japan Freight Railway Company, but runs on the rails of these passenger companies.

The Shinkansen Property Corporation is responsible for the leasing of the Shinkansen lines and facilities to the railway operators.

Hedjaz Jordan Railway (HJR) Aqaba Railway Corporation (ARC)

Gauge: 1,050mm (41.37in)
Extent: HJR 326km (202.47 miles), ARC 293km (181.95 miles)

HJR has struggled to survive since 1983, but some freight services were reintroduced in 1985 and also a passenger service between Amman and Zarqua in 1987, at which time it used five diesel-electric GE-built locomotives.

Kenya Railways (KR)

Gauge: 1,000mm (39.4in)
Extent: 2,650km (1,645.65 miles)

KR operates a main line from Mombasa through Nairobi to the Ugandan border, plus limited branch lines using a fleet of some 229 diesel locomotives.

North Korean Railway

Gauge: 1,435mm (56.54in)
Extent: over 4,000km (2,484 miles)
Electrification: 25kV 50Hz covering over half of the network.

The railways, like much of the country, have deteriorated over the past decade and are in urgent need of finance. However it appears that this is unlikely to become available in the immediate future.

Korean National Railways (KNR)

Gauge: 1,435 and 762mm (56.54 and 30.02in)
Extent: 3,074 and 47km (1,908.95 and 29.19 miles) respectively
Electrification: 411km (255.23 miles) at 25kV 60Hz ac

The main route runs between Pusan and Seoul and is double-tracked, but the rapid growth during the 1970s levelled off in the 1980s owing to competition from an improved and expanding road network. Locomotives include about 500 diesels, 100 electrics, and also 50 electric trainsets.

Luxembourg Railways (CFL)

Gauge: 1,438mm (55.32in)
Extent: 270km (167.67 miles)
Electrification: 218km (135.38 miles) at 25kV 50Hz ac and 19km (11.8 miles) at 3kV dc

CFL operates 20 electric Class 3600 Bo-Bo locomotives, as well as over 50 diesel-electrics.

MADAGASCAR

Société d'État Réseau National des Chemins de Fer Malagasy (RNCFM)

Gauge: 1,000mm (39.4in)
Extent: 883km (548.34 miles)

Lying predominantly in the central eastern region of the country, the network consists

Above: *an AD 16 B of RNCFM*

of a northern and a southern system. Traffic comprises about 650,000 freight tonnes (1,432.9 million lb) as well as 2.7 million passenger journeys. Locomotives include Alsthom-built Class BB 250 Bo-Bos.

Malawi Railways Ltd (MR)
Gauge: 1,067mm (42.04in)
Extent: 789km (489.97 miles)
A single track runs from near the Zambian border through Lilongwe, Blantyre and on to the border with Moçambique.

Malayan Railway
Administration (PKTM)
Gauge: 1,000mm (39.4in)
Extent: 1,639km (1,017.82 miles)
The main line runs from Singapore north through Kuala Lumpur to the seaport of Butterworth, and is linked with the State railways of Thailand for through services to Bankok, as is its second line, the 528km (327.89-mile) long east coast line, which also links to the Singapore-Butterworth line. PKTM's 150 diesel locomotives are a completely mixed bag, but in the 1980s Hitachi Class 24 Co-Cos were favoured.

Chemins de Fer du Mali (RCFM)
Gauge: 1,000mm (39.4in)
Extent: 641km (398.06 miles)
and 815km (506.12 miles)
Includes part of the former Dakar-Niger Railway; the RCFM has seen considerable increases in the past ten years, in both freight and passenger traffic, both of which have more than doubled.

Ferrocarriles Nationales de Mexico (FN de M)

Gauge: 1,435mm and 914mm (56.54 and 36.01in)
Extent: 15,095km and 39km (9,374 and 24.22 miles) respectively

In 1985, FN de M had an external debt of US$736 million, but traffic was increasing and with the Government writing off about half of this, the railway's large network is now in much better shape. Since 1985, new lines and electrification at 25kV 50Hz have begun, after many delays. The first orders for GE Type E 60 C 4,400kW Co-Co locomotives had been made ready for delivery as early as 1982. Meanwhile, about 1,500 diesel-electric locomotives are employed.

Above: *a Type CC diesel-electric locomotive, Mali 1988*

Below: *an E 1300 BB passenger locomotive of Moroccan Nationa. Railways, with a continuous rating of 4,000kW (5,360hp). These choppers are equipped with high-powered GTO thyristors*

Moroccan Railways (ONCFM)
Gauge: 1,435mm (56.54in)
Extent: 1,779km (1,104.76 miles)
Electrification: 794km at 3kV dc
An important freight network for transportation of minerals; the National Railway Corporation is a public industrial and commercial enterprise under the Ministry of Transport.

Moçambique State Railways (CFM)
Gauge: 1,067mm (42.04in)
Extent: 3,128km (1,942.49 miles)
Comprises five systems which link the coastal ports to the major towns of the hinterland. The largest is the southern system, which extends for 1,296km (804.81 miles).

Netherlands Railways (NS)
Gauge: 1,435mm (56.54in)
Extent: 2,971km (1,844.99 miles)
Electrification: 1,946km (1,208.47 miles) at 1.5kV dc
NS is a limited company, the shares of which are all held entirely by the State. Freight and passenger traffic are subsidised. There are close links between NS and air travel, with 75% of all NS stations providing access to Schipol airport, Amsterdam, either by direct train or with only one change of train. Track to train radio operates through the whole system, with messages contin-

uously recorded by Phillips voice-logging equipment. The locomotives include over 150 electric and twice as many diesels, plus locotractors, emus and dmus.

Above: *a bi-level push-pull trainset of NS*

Below: *an NS ICIII Bo-Bo emu, first introduced in 1977*

New Zealand Railways Corporation (NZR)

Gauge: 1,067mm (42.04in)
Extent: 4,266km (2,649.19 miles)
Electrification: 411km (255.23 miles) at 1.5kV dc and 411km (255.23 miles) at 25kV 50Hz ac

Deregulation of New Zealand's road transport industry in 1983 resulted in increased competition for the railways, and together with the downturn in the economy led to the establishment of the Railfreight system in April 1987, which now provides a far more cost-efficient service. NZR's first electric locomotives for the North Island Main Trunk railway line between Palmerston North and Bunnythorpe were Brush Electrical Bo-Bo-Bos with 4,350kW output capable of 105km/h (65.21mph) maximum speed.

DX class of NZR built by GE in the USA, taken at Raurimu Spiral, North Island, Main Trunk Railway

Nigerian Railway Corporation (NRC)

Gauge: 1,067 and 1,435mm (42.04 and 56.54in)
Extent: 3,505 and 51.2km (2,176.61 and 31.8 miles) respectively

The most sophisticated road and rail network in West Africa; the entire railway network is split into six divisions plus a headquarters based in Lagos. Locomotives include over 200 main-line diesels.

Norwegian State Railways (NSB)

Gauge: 1,435mm (56.54in)
Extent: 4,219km (2,620 miles)
Electrification: 2,443km (1,517.1 miles) at 15kV $16\frac{2}{3}$Hz ac

Intercity services from Oslo to Stavanger, Bergen and Trondheim were upgraded in 1990 with two daily trains in each direction, each one having improved onboard facilities and fewer stops. The trains cater for full-fare paying passengers only.

In addition, new tunnels on the Oslo to Bergen line have helped to reduce journey times. Motive power totals 178 electric locomotives and over 100 diesels.

Pakistan Railways (PR)
Gauge: 1,676, 1,000 and 762mm (66.03, 39.4 and 30.02in)
Extent: 7,718, 446 and 611km (4,792.88, 276.97 and 379.43 miles) respectively
Electrification: 290km (180.09 miles) of 1,676mm (66.03in) gauge at 25kV 50Hz ac
Since 1983 PR has made a big effort to attract increased passenger and freight traffic. An update plan included purchase of 105 diesel-electric locomotives plus passenger coaches and freight wagons including container wagons, and upgrading of track to take the increased weights and speeds. By the end of the five-year plan, a new locomotive factory had also been built with a production capability of 25 diesel-electric locomotives per year.

PARAGUAY

Ferrocaril Presidente Carlos Antonio Lopez
Gauge: 1,435mm (56.54in)
Extent: 441km (273.86 miles)
The only one of the four Paraguayan railways to carry any passengers; owned and operated by the Government, it is the largest of the four railways.

PERU

Empresa Nacional de Ferrocarriles del Peru (ENAFER)
Gauge: 1,435 and 914mm (56.54 and 36.01in)
Extent: 1,351 and 300km (839 and 186 miles) respectively
ENAFER was formed in 1972 when the Peruvian Corporation Railways were nationalised, together with the Central Railway and the Southern Railway, to carry some 3 million passengers and over 2.5 million tonnes (5,511.5 million lb) of freight per year.

Philippine National Railways (PNR)
Gauge: 1,067mm
Extent: 1,059km (657.64 miles)
Since 1979 much of the system has undergone considerable rehabilitation, and both passenger and freight traffic is again on the increase.

Polish State Railways (PKP)

Gauge: 1,435, 1,524mm (56.54, 60.05in) and also some minor extents of 1,000, 785, 750 and 600mm (39.4, 30.93, 29.55 and 23.64in)
Extent: 24,000 and 2,515km (14,904 and 1,561.82 miles)
Electrification: 11,000km (6,831 miles) at 3kV dc and 35km (21.74 miles) at 600V dc

During the 1980s PKP was one of the most intensively-used railway systems in the world and had the biggest traffic volume in Europe after the Soviet Union. In 1985, PKP opened its new Oder main line, 660km (409.86 miles) long. The track had been completely rebuilt and electrified and connects the industrial regions and coal mines with the Baltic ports. PKP intercity track route now covers 1,500km (913.5 miles), uniting 15 major centres and 40% of the population.

Portuguese Railways (CP)

Gauge: 1,668 and 1,000mm (65.72 and 39.4in)
Extent: 2,858 and 755km (1,774.82 and 468.86 miles) respectively
Electrification: 1,668mm gauge 434km (269.51 miles) at 25kV 50Hz ac, and 26km (16.15 miles) at 1.5kV dc

Until nationalisation in April 1975, CP had suffered serious neglect but even then it took another ten years before the Government made sufficient funds available to begin the rehabilitation of the existing infrastructure. By that time, CP was beginning to enjoy the benefits of greatly increased passenger traffic, particularly in the commuter areas of Lisboa and Oporto. CP has also recently been adding gradually to its fleet of locomotives, diesel and electric, for both the broad gauge and the narrow gauge, plus many more emus for its suburban services.

Romanian State Railways (CFR)

Gauge: 1,435, 610 and 762mm (56.54, 24.03 and 30.02in)
Extent: 10,515 and 568km (6,529.82 and 352.73 miles)
Electrification: 2,367km (1,469.91 miles) at 25kV 50Hz ac

Throughout the 1970s Romania had made a big effort to increase rail communications, and freight traffic in particular had shown a steady increase.

Electrified main lines are based on international traffic and while a large variety of diesel-hydraulic locomotives are employed, only two types of electric locomotives are used on the single-phase electrified lines, both built under licence from ASEA.

Saudi Government Railroad Organisation
Gauge: 1,435mm (56.54in)
Extent: 875km (543.38 miles)
Both freight and passenger traffic fell throughout the 1980s, despite improved track, faster scheduling and the purchase of more efficient locomotives. These are now serviced in a new workshop at Dammam, which caters for 78 main-line locomotives and 33 shunters with a maximum total capacity of 20 locomotives at any one time.

A GEC Alsthom-built 50kV thyristor-controlled heavy freight locomotive

Regie des Chemins de Fer du Sénégal (RCFS)
Gauge: 1,000mm (39.4in)
Extent: 905km (562 miles)
Sénégal's railway system comprises two basic main lines, which run from Dakar to St Louis and Linguère in the north-east and to the border with Mali in the east. Traffic is both freight and passenger, with over 30 million passenger journeys annually.

South Africa Transport Services (SATS)
Gauge: 1,065 and 610mm (41.96 and 24.03in)
Extent: 23,131 and 481km (14,364.35 and 298.7 miles)

respectively

Electrification: 6,000km (3,726 miles) at 3kV dc; 801km (497.42 miles) at 50kV ac; 2,220km (1,378.62 miles) at 25kV ac and 15km (9.32 miles) at dual 3kV dc/25kV ac

Both passenger and freight traffic peaked in 1984, before dropping sharply by the end of the 1980s. Coal and coke shipments comprise the bulk of the 90,000 million tonnes/km (125,193,600lb miles), while the passenger split is 30% main-line and 70% suburban and totals 700 million journeys.

SATS still operates over 600 steam locomotives alongside its 2,370 electric and over 1,500 diesel locomotives, which include a lot of General Motors South African-built Co-Co and Bo-Bo locomotives.

AD 16 B single cab of Spanish National Railways

Spanish National Railways (RENFE)

Gauge: 1,668, 1,000 and 1,435mm (65.72, 39.4 and 56.54in)

Extent: 12,721, 19 and 471km (7,899.74, 11.8 and 292.49 miles) respectively

Electrification: 1,668mm (65.72in) gauge 6,154km (3,821.63 miles) at 3kV dc, 48km (29.81 miles) at 1.5kV dc; 1,000mm (39.4in) gauge 19km (11.8 miles) at 1.5kV dc and 1,435mm (56.54in) gauge 471km at 25kV 50Hz ac and 3kV dc

Since 1985, the major events have been the spread of the 160km/h (99.36mph) intercity operation which has reduced the journey time for Madrid-Barcelona to six hours and 56 minutes for the 687km (426.63-mile) trip. The rapid upgrading between major cities was easily handled by RENFE's motive power, for which a substantial number of vehicles already existed, including 220 electric locomotives of Classes 269, 250 and 251, in addition to Class 354 Talgo diesels.

In October 1986, the decision was taken by the Government to build a new rail access to Andalusia and the tender for 24 Alta Velocidad Española (AVE) high-speed trains was opened in 1988. Later that year, the decision to adopt the standard European gauge of 1,435mm

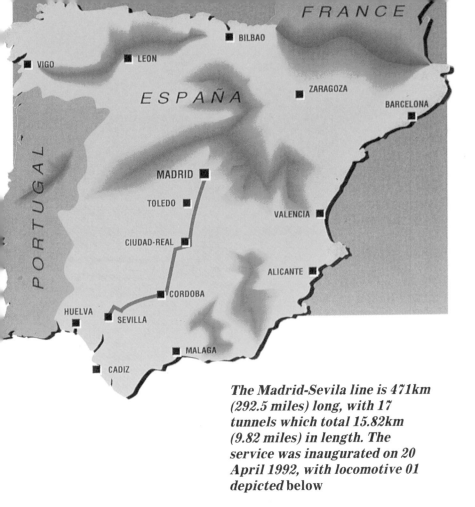

The Madrid-Sevila line is 471km (292.5 miles) long, with 17 tunnels which total 15.82km (9.82 miles) in length. The service was inaugurated on 20 April 1992, with locomotive 01 depicted below

AVE (Alta Velocidad Española 10-car train)

Railway: Spanish National Railways (RENFE)
Date: 1991
Type: high-speed multiple electric passenger locomotive
Gauge: 1,435mm (54.56in)
Length overall: 200m (656ft 2.4in)
Total weight: 421 tonnes (928,136lb)
Propulsion: 50Hz (25,000V) or 3,000V dc fed to two power cars of Bo-Bo type via overhead catenary through rectifiers and/or chopper control via eight three-phase synchronous self-commutated motors supplied by free turn-off thyristor invertors.
Maximum axle load: 17.2 tonnes (37,919lb)
Maximum speed: 300km/h (186.3mph)
History: in 1986, the Spanish Government began building a new rail line from Madrid to Sevila, a distance of 471km (292.49 miles). The initial order was for 24 AVE locomotives. The first of these, stemming from GEC Alsthom's successful TGV design, have adopted special features required by the Spanish network. The inaugural commercial service was run on 20 April 1992.

(56.54in) and to purchase the trainsets from GEC Alsthom was made. The first AVE train was delivered on 10 October 1991, and the inauguration of commercial service began on the Madrid-Sevila line on 20 April 1992. The line is 471km (292.49 miles) long with 17 tunnels totalling 15.82km (9.82 miles).

The AVE train has its origin in SNCF's TGV, with technical and aesthetic improvements to adapt it to the particular conditions of RENFE. These included special attention to cope with the tunnels and the 30% gradients encountered on the route. The AVE incorporates a new interior layout to provide increased distance between seats, an audio-video system at each passenger seat and a background music broadcasting system in each car. Facilities for wheelchairs are also improved, and provision for a nursery and children's play tables has been made in the 'family' compartment.

Above and below the main picture are the two power cars and eight passenger coaches, which have a total seating capacity of 329 with 116 in first class and 213 in second

Polished and at rest, AVE Nos 3 and 6 at Madrid

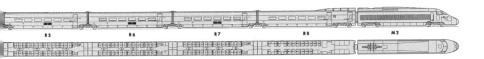

Sri Lanka Railways (SLR)

Gauge: 1,676 and 762mm (66.03 and 30.02in)
Extent: 1,394 and 59km (865.67 and 36.64 miles) respectively
Lines radiate from the centre at Colombo, going north along the coast to Illarankulam, south to Matara and east to the central highlands. Locomotives include 175 diesel plus 20 diesel trainsets.

Sudan Railways (SRC)

Gauge: 1,067mm (42.04in)
Extent: 4,786km (2,972.11 miles)
Since the mid-1980s much of the single-line track has been upgraded. SRC runs both steam and diesel locomotives.

Swaziland Railways (SR)

Gauge: 1,067mm (42.04in)
Extent: 370km (229.77 miles)
Only completed in the 1960s, SR runs 18 steam locomotives. These are leased from South Africa Transport Services.

Swedish State Railways (SJ)

Gauge: 1,435 and 891mm (54.56 and 35.11in)
Extent: 10,819 and 97km (6,718 and 60.24 miles) respectively
Electrification: 6,955km (4,319.06 miles) at 15kV $16\frac{2}{3}$Hz ac
Sweden maintains the largest European railway length per capita, with 1.5km (0.9315 mile) of track per 1,000 inhabitants.

It is treated as a social service, where the Government sets the fare scales and subsidises SJ to cover the deficit, with the majority of the network only carrying 8% of passenger traffic. Freight transport totals some 75,000 million tonnes/km (165,345,000 million lb). High-speed tilt-body trainsets were first ordered for the Stockholm to Gothenburg service in 1986, when SJ purchased 20 ASEA-built Series X2s each comprising a power car, four trailing cars and a driving trailer, and these provide a service over the 456km (283-mile) route of just under three hours.

A 1975 Class Rc4 Bo-Bo. The $16\frac{2}{3}$Hz 15,000V alternating current is fed via overhead catenary with step-down transformer and a thyristor control system

SWITZERLAND

The Class Re 4/4 above was introduced in 1964, to replace the 1944 Class AE 4/4

The railway network in Switzerland is not only complex but also very accessible, with 50% of the population living within 1km (0.621 mile) of a rail station, and services between major cities running half-hourly. Despite the problems of the terrain, the railway companies have always been to the fore of electric locomotion and technical development.

Swiss Federal Railways comprises:

Schweizerische Bundesbahnen (SBB)
Chemins de Fer Fédéraux Suisses (CFF)
Ferrovie Federali Svizzere (FFS)
Gauge: 1,435 and 1,000mm (56.54 and 39.4in)
Extent: 2,897 and 74km (1,799.04 and 45.95 miles) respectively
Electrification: 1,435mm (56.54in) gauge 2,897km (1,799.04 miles) at 15kV $16\frac{2}{3}$Hz ac and 1,000mm (39.4in) gauge 74km (45.95 miles) at 15kV $16\frac{2}{3}$Hz ac
SBB introduced a Bahn 2000 concept in 1986, basing improved services on eight city hubs fed from nearly 50 additional gateway stations. Improved services include upgrading tracks for higher speeds (200km/h/124.2mph) to combine reduced journey times with increased train frequency.

Other Swiss railways include:

Berne-Lötschberg-Simplon Railway (BLS)
Gauge: 1,435mm (56.54in)
Extent: 115km (71.42 miles)
Electrification: 115km (71.42 miles) at 15kV $16\frac{2}{3}$Hz ac
Centred on Berne, BLS controls 130km (80.73 miles) of other group railways, and operates throughout the system 55 electric locomotives.

Bernese Oberland Railways (BOB)
Gauge: 1,000mm (39.4in)
Extent: 24km (14.9 miles)
Electrification: 24km (14.9 miles) at 1.5kV dc
These details apply to the Berner Oberland-Bahnen railway, which is part of the BOB system, and is linked with Wengernalp-Bahn (WAB). (The latter runs an 800mm/31.52in gauge line immediately below the Jungfrau mountain chain.)

It is also linked with the Jungfraubahn (JB) on metre-gauge line that tunnels through the Jungfrau range and reaches a height of 3,405m (11,171ft 9.6in) above sea level. The JB is electrified at 1,100V 50Hz three-phase ac.

The BOB ABeh 4/4 railcar is Switzerland's most powerful dc motive power unit, capable of hauling loads of 101 tonnes (222,705lb) up 1 in 8.4 grades

Bodensee-Toggenburg Railway (BT)

Gauge: 1,435mm (56.54in)
Extent: 65.9km (40.92 miles)
Electrification: 65.9km (40.92 miles) at 15kV $16\frac{2}{3}$Hz ac
BT has only recently opened its first 1.2km (0.7452 mile) double-track section, and is part of the SBB Bahn 2000 scheme, for which a new traction and rolling stock programme was embarked upon.

Brig-Visp Zermatt Railway (BVZ)

Gauge: 1,000mm (39.4in)
Extent: 44km (27.32 miles)
Electrification: 44km (27.32 miles) at 11kV $16\frac{2}{3}$Hz ac

Emmental-Burgdorf-Thun Railway (EBT)

Gauge: 1,435mm (56.54in)
Extent: 71.2km (44.22 miles)
Electrification: 71.2km (44.22 miles) at 15kV $16\frac{2}{3}$Hz ac

Furka-Oberalp Railway (FO)

Gauge: 1,000mm (39.4in)
Extent: 100.4km (62.35 miles)
Electrification: 100.4km (62.35 miles) at 11kV $16\frac{2}{3}$Hz ac
FO is the important central link in the Swiss metre-gauge network.

Montreux-Oberland Bernois Railway (MOB)

Gauge: 1,000mm (39.4in)

Extent: 75.3km (46.76 miles)
Electrification: 75.3km (46.76 miles) at 860V dc
MOB took delivery of the popular 1,000kW G De 4/4 Bo-Bo locomotives in 1983 to haul its 'panoramic express'.

Rhaetian Railway (RhB)
Gauge: 1,000mm (39.4in)
Extent: 375km (232.88 miles)
Electrification: 276km (171.4 miles) at 11kV 16⅔Hz ac; 26.4km (16.39 miles) at 2.4kV dc; 60.8km (37.76 miles) at 1kV dc and 13km (8.07 miles) at 1.5kV dc
The system encompasses no fewer than 118 tunnels, which together with avalanche shelters extend to 39km (24.22 miles). The 498 bridges and viaducts total 12km (7.45 miles) in length.

South Eastern Railway
Gauge: 1,435mm (56.54in)
Extent: 46.67km (28.98 miles)
Electrification: 46.67km (28.98 miles) at 15kV 16⅔Hz ac
Jointly operates an important cross-country intercity passenger service together with the Swiss Federal and Bodensee-Toggenburg Railways.

SYRIA

Chemins de Fer Syriens (CFS)
Gauge: 1,435mm (56.54in)

Extent: 1,686km (1,047.01 miles)
CFS operates 173 diesel locomotives on its standard gauge system. The 246km (152.77 miles) of narrow gauge is operated by Chemins de Fer du Hedjaz. Main lines run from the Turkish border to the Lebanese border and from the oilfields of Kamechli as far as the port of Latakia.

Taiwan Railway Administration (TRA)
Gauge: 1,067mm (42.04in)
Extent: 1,075km (667.58 miles)
Electrification: 498km (309.26 miles) at 25kV 60Hz ac
The main system of transport on the island, TRA consists of three lines, the east line, the west line and the north line, and was completed in 1979, after six years of work. Motive power is mixed, with 38 steam, 112 electric and 179 diesel-electric locomotives.

Tanzanian Railways Corporation (TRC)
Gauge: 1,000mm (39.4in)
Extent: 2,600km (1,614.6 miles)
TRC still operates 59 steam locomotives alongside 112 diesels. Freight traffic is about 1 million tonnes (2,204.6 million lb) and passenger journeys 3 million.

Above: *a TZR V30C Co-Co 2,388kW (3,200hp) diesel-electric*

Above right: *a GEC Alsthom-built AD 24C of RSR*

Tanzania-Zambia Railway Authority (TZR)

Gauge: 1,067mm (42.04in)
Extent: 1,860km (1,155.06 miles), of which 891km (553.31 miles) are in Zambia

Constructed since 1967, with finance from the People's Republic of China. Tracklaying was completed in 1975, at which time 93 of the projected 147 stations had been completed. Commercial operations began the following year for both passengers and freight, although it is still operating well below envisaged capacity.

State Railway of Thailand (RSR)

Gauge: 1,000mm (39.4in)

Extent: 3,735km (2,319.44 miles)

Three of RSR's intercity passenger services were privatised as early as 1985, using Japanese-built railcars delivered that year; they were leased to private companies for services operating between Bankok and Phitsanulok, Surin and Khan Kaen. Motive power includes 184 diesel-electrics, 50 diesel-hydraulics and some steam locomotives.

Tunisian National Railways (SNCFT)

Gauge: 1,435, 1,000 and 1,050mm (56.54, 39.4 and 41.37in)
Extent: 465 and 1,650km (288.77 and 1,024.65 miles)

SNCFT remains strongly positioned with 60% of passenger and 70% of national freight traffic. It deploys 200 main line and shunting diesel locomotives and 50 diesel railcar units, which are being gradually upgraded despite a stagnation in both passenger and freight traffic.

Turkish State Railways (TCDD)
Gauge: 1,435mm (56.54in)
Extent: 8,169km (5,072.95 miles)
Electrification: 291km (180.71 miles) at 25kW 50Hz ac
Freight movements stand at about 15 million tonnes (33,069 million lb), and passenger journeys at about 140 million and include the popular first-class only Blue Train series, which operates out of Ankara.

Uganda Railway Corporation (URC)
Gauge: 1,000mm (39.4in)
Extent: 1,286km (798.61 miles)
The network has been steadily upgraded since 1980, and now operates an impressive fleet of 67 diesel locomotives.

USSR

Soviet Union Railways (SZD)
Gauge: 1,520, 600-1,435mm (59.89, 23.64-56.54in)
Extent: 145,668 and 2,608km (90,459.83 and 1,619.57 miles)
Electrification: 28,280km (17,561.88 miles) at 25 or 2 × 25kV 50Hz ac and 27,309km (16,958.89 miles) at 3kV dc
The Ministry of Railway Transport continues to control SZD and has responsibility for about

75% of freight movements. Approximately 90% of passenger volume is short-haul suburban traffic. In real terms this meant 4,400 million tonnes of freight (9,700,240 million lb) and over 4 billion passengers in 1990.

The Ministry incorporates 32 railroads, 174 railway sections, and underground lines which total 500km (310.5 miles). It is responsible for four million people, of which half are employed directly with transportation. An effort to raise speeds for high-speed trains from 140km/h to 160km/h (86.94 to 99.36mph) is being targeted at 9,000km (5,589 miles) of track, including the prestige routes out of Moscow, with a maximum speed of 200km/h (124.2mph) having been realised on the Moscow-St Petersburg line.

Today's fleet includes twelve axle two-unit ac electric Class B85 and B86 locomotives, and induction traction motors, 2TE 136 diesel locomotives with ac/dc electrical transmission and 4,477kW (6,000hp) per unit plus T3M7 diesel shunters.

On suburban services EP29 and EP30 dc electric trains with regenerative braking are also employed.

Below: *dc electric locomotive model YC4 with a 5,500kW power output and a maximum speed of 160km/h (99.36mph)*

Right: *short-haul shunting diesel loco T3M7 has a power rating of 1,470kW (2,000hp) and a mass of 180 tonnes (396,828lb)*

UNITED KINGDOM

British Rail (BR)

Gauge: 1,435mm (56.54in)
Extent: 16,729km (10,388.71 miles)
Electrification: 2,042.2km (1,268.21 miles) at 25kV 50Hz ac; 1,803.6km (1,120.04 miles) at 750V dc third rail

The most talked-about railway project of recent years has been the Channel Tunnel, and as this book goes to press the official opening of the Tunnel is due. The Tunnel complex comprises a service tunnel of 4.5m (14ft 9.12in) diameter connected every 375m (1,230ft 4.56in) by cross-passages on both sides of two railway tunnels 7.3m (23ft 11.4in) in diameter. The tunnels run for 50km (31.05 miles) under the Channel bed, with the terminals at Cheriton near Folkestone, Kent, and Frethon, near Calais in France.

The service, operated by Eurotunnel, will cover road vehicles such as cars, coaches and lorries carried on specially-designed shuttle trains, while BR and SNCF will operate international passenger and freight trains operating as through services between the UK and continental Europe. Despite many disputes and delays, the Tunnel is now due to open following trial agreements made in December 1993 and we can only wait to see what effect this vast project will have upon future international rail traffic.

Meanwhile, the British Government is preparing to spend some £200 million (US $300 million) on the privatisation of BR, not altogether a popular move when one considers the serious financial plight of the vast majority of the world's railways. It can only be imagined that the Government will have to continue to subsidise the operations of a considerable section of the network in order to maintain any decent standard of service. It also comes at a time when BR has experienced especially in the Network South-East section, a downturn in passenger traffic; a disappointment after the 1980s had proved to be something of a success on both the passenger and the freight traffic fronts.

BR operates some 2,500 diesel locomotives, 250 electric locomotives, 200 HST power and 750 trailer cars, 3,300 locomotive-hauled passenger cars, 1,650 non-passenger cars, 2,750 emu and 7,000 emu cars, and 34,000 freight wagons.

During the 1980s, BR took

A Western (D1000) Class of 1961

delivery of Class 43, 56, 58, 59, 60, 89, 90 and 91 diesel locomotives, Class 141, 142, 143, 144, 150, 151, 155, 156 and 158 diesel multiple-units and Class 314, 315, 317, 318, 319, 321, 442, 455, 457, 488, 489, 507 and 508 electric multiple-units.

Class 87 Bo-Bo

Country of origin: UK
Railway: British Railways (BR)
Date: 1973
Type: mixed-traffic electric locomotive
Gauge: 1,435mm (54.56in)
Length overall: 17.83m (58ft 6in)
Total weight: 83 tonnes (182,930lb)
Propulsion: 50Hz (25,000V) alternating current fed via overhead catenary with step-down transformer and solid-state rectifiers to four 932kW (1,250hp) fully spring-borne traction motors, driving the axles by gearing and ASEA hollow-axle flexible drives.
Maximum axle load: 20.75 tonnes (45,735lb)
Tractive effort: 238kN (58,000lb)
Maximum speed: 160km/h (100mph)

Above right: *Class 87 No 87009 City of Birmingham*

Centre: *a Class 141 of 1983*

Below: *Intercity HST Class 254 No 43049 at Chesterfield in July 1990*

HST 125 ten-car trainset

Country of origin: UK
Railway: British Railways (BR)
Date: 1978
Type: diesel-electric high-speed train
Gauge: 1,435mm (54.56in)
Length overall: 219.584m (720ft 5in)
Total weight: 383 tonnes (844,132lb); adhesive weight 142 tonnes (308,560lb)
Propulsion: one 1,680kW (2,250hp) supercharged Paxman Valenta 12RP200L V12 engine with integral alternator in each of two driving motor vans, each engine feeding current to sets of four traction motors mounted in the bogie frames
Maximum axle load: 17.5 tonnes (38,570lb)
Maximum speed: 200km/h (125mph)
History: the HST 125 was Britain's nationalised rail system's first major passenger train success story. Planned as a series of 132 trains, it was intended that they should cover the main non-electrified routes of British Railways with a network of 200km/h (125mph) trains. The number was reduced to 95, but provided a dense and comprehensive high-speed service.

UNITED STATES OF AMERICA

The USA was the first nation to transfer to road from rail, and thereby to commit rail to decay; but this is all set to revert at the end of the twentieth century as the roads become more and more congested, making the journey by car slower.

The early 1990s riots in Los Angeles have brought the problem to a head; it is difficult to get people out of their cars and back onto the trains, but it is happening in LA with a massive

The biggest passenger boom in the USA peaked in 1944, when the Pennsylvania Railroad was running 139 of these streamlined GGI 2-6-6-2 locomotives, which used 25Hz (15,000V) medium-frequency ac, fed via overhead catenary with step-down transformer to twelve 305kW (410hp) traction motors, each pair driving a main axle

vote from the electorate for a new mass-transport system. Car sales are slumping, and just maybe the rebirth of rail is about to take place.

Note: because of the limited space available, coverage of rail in the USA is restricted to Class 1 railroads, defined as those with a turnover of over £54.66 million (US$82 million).

The Alaska Railroad

Gauge: 1,435mm (56.54in)
Extent: 846km (525.37 miles)
Heavily reliant on Electro Motive GP diesel locomotives, the corporation runs a single-track main line of 756km (469.48 miles) from the ports of Seward and Whittier then northward through Anchorage and Denali National Park to Fairbanks and eastward to Eielson.

The first purchase of Amtrak was for these F40PH diesel-electric passenger locos

National Railroad Passenger Corporation (Amtrak)

Gauge: 1,435mm (56.54in)
Extent: 557km (345.9 miles)
Electrification: 554.6km (344.41 miles) at 11kV 25Hz ac
Created in October 1970, when the Rail Passenger Service Act came into force, services began in May 1971, thus establishing the first nationwide passenger service in the USA to be under one management. Amtrak is heavily reliant on the good condition of infrastructure now owned by the private freight operators, over which the passenger services run. Amtrak employs over 20,000 people in 44 States and the New York to Washington service alone carries 18,000 passengers daily; total annual passenger journeys top 20 million.

Boston and Maine Corporation

Gauge: 1,435mm (56.54in)
Extent: 2,532km (1,572.37 miles)
Essentially a freight haulage company, the major lines of which run north and west from Boston through the States of Maine, New Hampshire, Vermont, Massachusetts and on into New York State. Locomotives include 114 line-haul and 48 switchers, all diesel-electric.

Burlington Northern (BN)

Gauge: 1,435mm (56.54in)
Extent: 44,381.8km (27,561.1 miles)
Formed in 1970 as the result of a merger between the Chicago, Burlington & Quincy Railroad, the Great Northern Railway, the Northern Pacific Railway and the Spokane, Portland and Seattle Railway, this large network spanned 19 States, plus two Canadian provinces, stretching from the Great Lakes to the Pacific coast and south to the Gulf of Mexico.

Following the subsequent merger in 1980 with the St Louis-San Francisco Railway Company, a further six States were added to the network, which then became the largest railroad in the USA, with the transportation of coal its largest source of freight revenue. Burlington uses unit trains of between three and six locomo-tives and often consisting of over 100 hopper or gondola cars, each capable of holding 100 tonnes (224,000lb) of coal. It is therefore no surprise to find BN has 2,000 freight line-haul locomotives, 25 passenger, 300 multi-purpose, 230 switchers and 60,000 freight cars.

Chicago and North Western Transportation Company (C & NW)

Gauge: 1,435mm (56.54in)
Extent: 11,288km (7,010 miles)
The railroad was incorporated in 1970, and is engaged primarily in hauling rail freight traffic in nine midwest States. The company also handles freight traffic in the Chicago metropolitan area. The heaviest traffic is found on the 804km (499.28-mile) long line between Chicago and Council Bluffs, accounting for 46% of all freight traffic. An important oddity of the C & NW is that it is the only US railroad to operate trains on the left-hand track rather than the right.

*Top: **Burlington Northern's EMD-built Pioneer Zephyr, the first diesel-powered passenger locomotive in North America***

*Below: **Conrail GE C40-8 wide-cab locomotive just west of downtown Philadelphia***

Conrail

Gauge: 1,435mm (56.54in)
Extent: 19,005km (11,802.11 miles)

Operating since April 1976, Conrail was set up as a private profit-making corporation by an Act of Congress. It provides the most comprehensive freight service in the northeast and mid-west, operating in 15 States. It services some 250 coal mines and also operates a comprehensive 'Just-in-time' service for the automobile industry, collecting parts for delivery to assembly lines at the beginning of the next working day. In 1987, together with Santa Fe, Conrail introduced the fastest coast-to-coast service for intermodal traffic of 76 hours.

CSX Transportation Inc

Gauge: 1,435mm (56.54in)
Extent: 39,937km (24,800.88 miles)

The result of a merger between the Chessie System Inc and Seaboard Coast Line Industries in 1980, it serves 21 States plus the District of Columbia. Since 1986, CSX has had control of its major intermodal customer Sea-Land, giving it access to Sea-Land's terminals all over the world and, more importantly, control of a major container shipping line.

Delaware and Hudson Railroad Company (D & H)

Gauge: 1,435mm (56.54in)
Extent: 2,734km (1,697.81 miles)

By no means one of the largest railroads in North America, the D & H operates 140 locomotives and 5,000 freight cars and records over 6,334.31 million tonne/km (4,000 million ton miles) of freight annually.

The Denver and Rio Grande Western Railroad Company

Gauge: 1,435mm (56.54in)
Extent: 3,848km (2,389.61 miles)

The railroad operates from Denver to Pueblo in the east, Salt Lake City and Ogden to the west, and was established in 1969. In 1984, the Anschutz Corporation acquired the line. Now the fast express intermodal service operated by reduced crews runs the 917km (569.46 miles) between Denver and Salt Lake City overnight in 14 hours. Rolling stock includes over 300 diesel-electric locomotives and 10,000 freight cars.

Florida East Coast Railway Company

Gauge: 1,435mm (56.54in)
Extent: 859km (533.44 miles)

The system's main line is the trunk route from Jacksonville to Miami so essential to its profitability. It has 65 line-haul locomotives and 2,500 freight cars.

Illinois Central Gulf Railroad
Gauge: 1,435mm (56.54in)
Extent: 5,950km (3,694.95 miles)
Electrification: 64.5km (40.05 miles) at 1.5kV dc
Electrification is confined to the Chicago commuter area, where 200 bi-level emus are operated, and yet the system operates throughout eight States ranging from the Great Lakes to the Gulf of Mexico. Route extent was cut continuously throughout the 1970s and 1980s, while IC Industries sought a merger partner for the Railroad. IC Industries provides two-thirds of all the railroad's traffic, and locomotives total 700-plus diesels, and in excess of 30,000 freight cars.

Kansas City Southern Line
Gauge: 1,435mm (56.54in)
Extent: 2,686km (1,668 miles)
Main freight traffic comprises chemicals from the Gulf Coast refineries and chemical plants, forest products and coal, in addition to intermodal business between New Orleans and Dallas. Some 275 diesel locomotives are employed, together with over 7,000 freight cars.

Missouri-Kansas-Texas Railroad Company (MKT)
Gauge: 1,435mm (56.54in)
Extent: 3,929km (2,439.91 miles)
Operating in the States of Missouri, Kansas, Oklahoma, Texas, Nebraska and Iowa from 1983, it also runs a service between Kansas City and Omaha, Lincoln and Council Bluffs over lines belonging to other railroads. Main freight traffic includes wheat, lumber, steel, coal and automobiles, but suffered in 1980 when Burlington Northern merged with Frisco and again in 1982 when Union Pacific consolidated with Missouri Pacific, creating greatly increased competition and leading finally to the Missouri Pacific takeover of MKT.

Missouri Pacific Railroad (Mo Pac)
Gauge: 1,435mm (56.54in)
Extent: 16,878km (10,481.24 miles)
Mo Pac operates throughout 12 midwestern and southern States, reaching approximately one third of the area of the USA and one fifth of the population. A major key to its success has been that it connects to nearly all of the major US railroads and at the important junctions such as Chicago, Kansas City, Pueblo, Colorado, Memphis, New Orleans and at El Paso to the railroads of Mexico, and Canadian railroads via Chicago and Kansas. In addition to these important

connections, the network also serves 12 ports on the Gulf Coast. In 1982, following the merger of parent companies, Mo Pac became a sister company of Union Pacific.

Norfolk Southern Corporation (NS)

Gauge: 1,435mm (56.54in)
Extent: 28,198km (17,510.96 miles)
Coal, coke, and iron dominate the NS freight operation, with long-term low price for high volume coal contracts from some 200 companies accounting for 73% of its coal movements. NS was established in 1982 as a holding company to control the merger of the Norfolk and Western and Southern Railways which had been prompted by the formation of CSX. The newly-formed fleet totalled 2,230 diesel locomotives and 133,000 freight cars.

Pittsburgh & Lake Erie Railroad Company

Gauge: 1,435mm (56.54in)
Extent: 650km (403.65 miles)
The company was originally part of New York Central, then Penn Central, before buying its independence in 1979 with the help of external finance. Heavily dependent on the steel industry, which accounted for 75% of revenue, the railroad was now financially secure and only operated 38 line-haul diesel locomotives.

Atchison, Topeka and Santa Fe Railway Company (Santa Fe Railway)

Gauge: 1,435mm (56.54in)
Extent: 19,108km (11,866.07 miles)
A major restructuring began in 1986, with the intention of cutting the network's extent by 5,000km (3,105 miles) of track, together with the yards, 8,000 freight cars, 200 locomotives and over 4,000 employees. Of the latter, 800 went within the first two months of the programme's inception, leaving a total workforce of 22,400, down 12,500 from 1980. At the same time, Santa Fe entered into an agreement with CP Rail and the Soo Line for the provision of a better service between Canada and the USA. Prior to the rationalisation programme, Santa Fe operated 1,710 line-haul and 42 switcher diesel locomotives and 46,226 freight cars.

Soo Line Railroad Company

Gauge: 1,435mm (56.54in)
Extent: 12,465km (7,740.77 miles)
A subsidiary of CP, it absorbed the Milwaukee Road in 1985 to create one of the largest US networks, extending from east

to west, Lake Michigan to North Dakota, and south as far as Kansas City. Main traffic is comprised of intermodal business and Soo operates some 50 dedicated intermodal trains a week, 33 of which ply the 600km (372.6-mile) Chicago to Twin Cities corridor. Soo operates over 500 diesel locomotives and 17,000 freight cars.

Southern Pacific Transportation Company (SP)

Gauge: 1,435mm (56.54in)
Extent: 15,633km (9,708.09 miles)
This large network operates over 1,700 line-haul and 450 switcher diesel locomotives and some 42,500 freight cars, employed in a wide variety of services covering most major commodity groups. Automatic handling facilities include a 242.8ha (600-acre) site at Marne in the eastern Los Angeles Basin, capable of storing up to 3,700 vehicles and providing unloading capacity for 80 multi-level railcars. It opened in 1985, and a year later was already handling 21,000 vehicles per month. A second such facility exists at Phoenix.

Intermodal services include 'sprint' type with the introduction in 1983 of the new Texas Overnight Piggyback Express using 15-car trains with one locomotive operated by a two-man crew for the 400km (248.4-mile) Houston to Dallas journey.

Union Pacific Railroad Company (UP)

Gauge: 1,435mm (56.54in)
Extent: (including Missouri Pacific) 34,458km (21,398.42 miles)

UP itself services 21 States, connecting the major Pacific coast and Gulf ports with all of the key midwest gateways, through which UP has reciprocal arrangements with 32 other railroads to avoid breaking up trains.

Some 80,000 freight cars carry coal and coke products, soda ash and chemicals, grain, aggregates, steel and ores, products, foodstuffs, automobiles and automotive parts and intermodal. Main-line track accounts for over 20,000km (12,240 miles). UP power is provided by 2,700 diesel-electric locomotives, including over 700 EMD-built 2,238kW (3,000hp) SD-40 and SD-40-2 line-haul freight locomotives.

URUGUAY

State Railways Administration (AFE)

Gauge: 1,435mm (56.54in)
Extent: 2,991km (1,857.41 miles)

Following a downturn in traffic at the beginning of the 1980s, by the middle of the decade only about half of AFE's motive power or rolling stock was available for use, owing to its terrible state of disrepair. AFE sought to correct this by modernisation over the next five years, seeking new track of 50kg/m (120.61lb/yd) rail, new traction and rolling stock and rehabilitation of workshops.

Previous page: *SD 40-2 locos built by EMD for Union Pacific were the most popular metal ever built by EMD*

Below: *Union Pacific had 47 of these Class DD40AX 'Centennial' heavy freight diesel-electrics*

Below: *State Railways Administration's BB 925 locomotive No 820, built by GEC Alsthom, is a new acquisition to its fleet*

Venezuelan State Railways (IAFE)

Gauge: 1,435mm (56.54in)
Extent: 362.8km (225.3 miles)
By 1987, only 264km (163.94 miles) of main line from Puerto Caballo to Barguisameto was operational, and construction plans have been continually delayed and revised downwards. However, work has now begun on several main and branch lines, along with plans for electrification to provide rapid-transit facilities. Motive power is provided by just seven diesel locomotives.

Yugoslav Railways (JZ)

The extent of services and of serviceable track is not now clear, owing to the continuing civil war, but we do know how things looked prior to the break-up of the republic:
Gauge: 1,435mm (56.54in)
Extent: 9,422km (5,851.06 miles)
Electrification: 2,720km (1,689.12 miles) at 25kV 50Hz ac and 755km (468.86 miles) at 3kV dc (early electrification)
The early electrified route included the Zagreb-Rijeka route, which was to be converted to 25kV 50Hz. At the same time there were plans to upgrade the locomotive fleet, which still included over 100 steam locomotives, together with 500 electric, 800 diesels, 120 emus and 250 dmus.

Société Nationale des Chemins de Fer Zaïrois (SNCZ)

Gauge: 1,067, 1,000, 615 and 600mm (42.04, 39.4, 24.23 and 23.64in)
Extent: 3,884, 125, 136 and 1,023km (2,411.96, 77.63, 84.46 and 635.28 miles) respectively
Electrification: 1,067mm (42.04in) gauge 858km (532.82 miles) at 25kV 50Hz
SNCZ was created in 1974 by the merger of five former railways, and the resultant mix of gauges, traction and rolling stock of varying condition meant that perhaps 40% of wagons were immobilised and freight traffic was falling, while demand for passenger traffic continued to grow steadily.

Above: *Type U20C 1,604kW (2,150bhp) diesel-electric of Zambian Railways*

Right: *D10A locomotive of NRZ pulling a mixed goods train*

Zambian Railways Ltd (ZR)
Gauge: 1,067mm (42.04in)
Extent: 1,266km (786.19 miles)
Formerly part of the Rhodesian Railways, the ZR system was segregated in 1976. Current freight traffic is a steady five million tonnes (11,023 million lb), while passenger traffic fell throughout the 1980s and is now well below two million journeys. The mainstay traction power is provided by General Electric and Krupp-built Type U20C diesel-electric locomotives.

National Railways of Zimbabwe (NRZ)
Gauge: 1,067mm (42.04in)
Extent: 3,394km (2,107.67 miles)
Electrification: 311km (193.13 miles) at 25kV 50Hz ac
The NRZ system connects with lines from Moçambique, South Africa, Zambia and Botswana, where it was originally responsible for operating the through services. Freight traffic has remained steady, but passenger traffic showed a healthy increase throughout the 1980s, aided by the first 308km (191.27 miles) of electrification in 1983.

INDEX